CONCILIUM

THEOLOGY IN THE AGE OF RENEWAL

CONCILIUM

CONCILIUM / VOL. 15

MORAL THEOLOGY

WAR
POVERTY
FREEDOM

THE CHRISTIAN RESPONSE

Volume 15

CONCILIUM
theology in the age of renewal

PAULIST PRESS
NEW YORK, N.Y. / GLEN ROCK, N.J.

Copyright © 1966 by
Paulist Fathers, Inc. and *Stichting Concilium*

All Rights Reserved
Nothing contained in this publication shall be duplicated and/or made public by means of print, photography, microfilm, or in any other manner, without the previous consent of *Paulist Press* and *Stichting Concilium*.

Library of Congress Catalogue Card Number: 66-24233

Suggested Decimal Classification: 261.8

BOOK DESIGN: Claude Ponsot

Paulist Press assumes responsibility for the accuracy of the English translations in this Volume.

PAULIST PRESS
EXECUTIVE OFFICES: 304 W. 58th Street, New York, N.Y. and 21 Harristown Road, Glen Rock, N.J.
Executive Publisher: John A. Carr, C.S.P.
Executive Manager: Alvin A. Illig, C.S.P.
Asst. Executive Manager: Thomas E. Comber, C.S.P.

EDITORIAL OFFICES: 304 W. 58th Street, New York, N.Y.
Editor: Kevin A. Lynch, C.S.P.
Managing Editor: Urban P. Intondi

Printed and bound in the United States of America by
The Colonial Press Inc., Clinton, Mass.

CONTENTS

PART III

DO-C DOCUMENTATION CONCILIUM

PART I
ARTICLES

John Courtney Murray, S.J./*Woodstock, Md.*

The Declaration on Religious Freedom

The *Declaration on Religious Freedom* is a document of very modest scope. It is concerned only with the juridico-social order and with the validity, in that order, of a human and civil right to the free exercise of religion. The right is founded on the dignity of the human person; its essential requirement is that man in society should be free from all constraint or hindrance, whether legal or extra-legal, in what concerns religious belief, worship, witness and practice, both private and public. The structure of a rational argument for this right is briefly sketched; norms for legitimate limitation of the exercise of the right are laid down; the duty of government to protect and foster the free exercise of religion in society is affirmed. Then the implications of religious freedom for all Churches and religious communities are set forth in some detail. Thereafter the human right to religious freedom is considered under the light of revelation.

The intention of this section is simply to show that a harmony exists between religious freedom in the juridico-social sense, and Christian freedom in the various senses of this latter concept as they emerge from Scripture and from the doctrine of the Church. The Declaration merely suggests that the two kinds of freedom are related; it does not undertake to specify more closely what their precise relationship is. The conclusion of the Declaration

3

is a pastoral exhortation to the faithful and a respectful appeal to the conscience of mankind, urging the value of religious freedom, and of religion itself, in the world today.

The Declaration therefore does not undertake to present a full and complete theology of freedom. This would have been a far more ambitious task. It would have been necessary, I think, to develop four major themes: (1) the concept of Christian freedom—the freedom of the People of God—as a participation in the freedom of the Holy Spirit, the principal agent in the history of salvation, by whom the children of God are "led" (Rom. 8, 14) to the Father through the incarnate Son; (2) the concept of the freedom of the Church in her ministry, as a participation in the freedom of Christ himself, to whom all authority in heaven and on earth was given and who is present in his Church to the end of time (cf. Matt. 28, 18. 20); (3) the concept of Christian faith as man's free response to the divine call issued, on the Father's eternal and gracious initiative, through Christ, and heard by man in his heart where the Spirit speaks what he has himself heard (cf. John 16, 13-15); (4) the juridical concept of religious freedom as a human and civil right, founded on the native dignity of the human person who is made in the image of God and therefore enjoys, as his birthright, a participation in the freedom of God himself.

This would have been, I think, a far more satisfactory method of procedure, from the theological point of view. In particular, it would have been in conformity with the disposition of theologians today to view issues of natural law within the concrete context of the present historico-existential order of grace. Moreover, the doctrine presented would have been much richer in content. There were, however, decisive reasons why the Council could not undertake to present this full theology of freedom.

1. The Declaration is the only conciliar document that is formally addressed to the world at large on a topic of intense secular as well as religious interest. Therefore, it would have been inept for the Declaration to begin with doctrines that can be known only by revelation and accepted only by faith.

2. What the world at large, as well as the faithful within the Church, wants to know today is the stand of the Church on religious freedom as a human and civil right. It would be idle to deny that the doctrine of the Church, as formulated in the 19th century, is somewhat ambiguous in itself, out of touch with contemporary reality and a cause of confusion among the faithful and of suspicion throughout large sectors of public opinion.

3. The theological structure of the argument, as proposed above, would give rise to historical and theological problems which are still matters of dispute among theologians. There is, for instance, the problem of the exact relationship between Christian freedom and religious freedom. There is, furthermore, the whole problem of the development of doctrine, from *Mirari vos* to *Dignitatis humanae personae*.

4. Christian freedom, as the gift of the Holy Spirit, is not exclusively the property of the members of the visible Church, any more than the action of the Spirit is confined within the boundaries of the visible Church. This topic is of great ecumenical importance, but the discussion of it would have to be nice in every respect, and therefore impossible in a brief document.

5. Finally, there was a serious consideration of pastoral prudence. Christian freedom is indeed asserted over against all earthly powers (cf. Acts 4, 19-20; 5, 29); in this sense it prompted the witness of the martyrs. It is, however, also asserted within the Church; in this sense it is the warrant for charismatic ministries, and it is also the basis of prudent protest when the exercise of authority goes beyond legitimate bounds. As everyone knows, however, the issue of freedom within the Church is neuralgic today, as indeed it was when Paul wrote to the Galatians (cf. Gal. 5, 13). The issue is also highly complicated. It would have been imprudent, therefore, to raise this issue directly in a brief conciliar document. Hence the Declaration is at pains to distinguish sharply the issue of religious freedom in the juridico-social order from the larger issue of Christian freedom. The disastrous thing would be to confuse the two distinct issues. Obviously, the issue of Christian freedom—its basis, its meaning,

its exercise and its limits—will have to be clarified by free discussion, conducted carefully and patiently in a sustained dialogue between pastors and people over many years. However, this dialogue will be the more successful now that the Declaration has settled the lesser issue of the free exercise of religion in civil society.

Narrow though its scope may be, the Declaration is nonetheless a document of considerable theological significance. This will become apparent if the document is considered in the light of the two great historical movements of the 19th century, both of which were bitterly opposed by the Church.

I
THE SECULARITY OF SOCIETY AND STATE

The first movement was from the sacral conception of society and State to the secular conception. The sacral conception had been the heritage of medieval Christendom and, in a far more ambiguous form, of the ancien régime. For our purposes here, two of its characteristics should be briefly noted. First, the Christian world—or at least the Catholic nation—was considered to be somehow enclosed within the Church, which was herself the one Great Society. Second, the religious prerogative of the prince extended to a care of the religion of his subjects and a care of their religious unity as essential to their political unity. (This religious prerogative of political rule was interpreted in a variety of more or less arbitrary ways, but these details need not detain us here.)

The 19th century saw the break with this conception of the sacrality of society and State, and a movement toward their secularity. As everybody knows, the Church—both in Rome and in the so-called Catholic nations—opposed this movement with all the forces at her command. The reason was obvious. After the revolution in continental Europe (the new Federal Republic of the United States presents an altogether different case), the term of the historical movement was not a proper secularity of society and State. What emerged was the laicized State of rationalist or atheist inspiration, whose function was the laicization of society. In effect, what emerged was the ancien régime turned upside down, as Alexis de Tocqueville noted at the time. One might properly regard the Law of Separation (December 9, 1905) of the Third French Republic as the legislative symbol of the new order.

The Church could not in principle accept this new order in its premises, in its ethos, or even in its institutions, primary among which was the institution of the so-called "liberty of cult". Furthermore, the Church did not in fact do a work of discernment of the signs of the times in order to discover, beneath the transitory historical forms assumed by the new movement, the true and valid dynamisms that were at work.

The overt revolt was against the sacrality of society and State as symbolized by the union of throne and altar. Few historians today would deny that this conception and its institutional symbol, for all their venerable antiquity, had become archaistic in the world of modernity. However, the true underlying direction of the new movement was toward a proper and legitimate secularity of society and State. In the depths, where the hidden factors of historical change were operative, what was really going on was a work of differentiation, which is always a work of growth and progress. Civil society was seeking differentiation from the religious community, the Church. The political functions of secular rule were being differentiated from the religious functions of ecclesiastical authority. The trouble was that this work of orderly progress was disrupted and deflected, as so often happens in history.

Chiefly to blame was the disastrous law of contradiction—that desire to deny and destroy the past which was the very essence of Enlightenment rationalism (whereby it aroused the bitter antipathy, for instance, of Edmund Burke). What appeared on the surface, therefore, was not progress but simply revolution. Society as civil was not simply being differentiated from society as religious; the two societies were being violently separated, and civil society was being stripped of all religious substance. The order of civil law and political jurisdiction was not simply being differentiated from the order of moral law and ecclesiastical jurisdiction; a complete rupture was made between the two orders of law and the two authorities, and they were set at hostile variance, each with the other. Society and State were not invested with their due secularity; they were roughly clothed in the alien garments of continental laicism. At this horrid specter, stalking across the Europe of the Middle Ages, the Church in the person of Piux IX hurled her unmitigated anathema.

Leo XIII first began to discern whither the deep currents of history were setting. In response, he restored to its proper centrality, and also developed, the traditional truth that Gelasius I had sought to enforce upon the Emperor Anastasius in 494 A.D.: "Two there are, august Emperor, whereby this world is ruled by sovereign right (*principaliter*), the sacred authority of the priesthood and the royal power." However, Leo XIII transcended the historically conditioned medieval conception of the two powers in the one society called Christendom—a conception that, in debased form, had persisted under the ancien régime, with its Gallicanism and its famous device: "One faith, one law, one king." In a series of eight splendid texts, stretching from *Arcanum* (1880) to *Pervenuti* (1920), Leo XIII finally made it clear that there are two distinct societies, two distinct orders of law, as well as two distinct powers. This was the ancient affirmation in a new mode of understanding—an authentic development of doctrine. On this basis, Leo XIII was able to accomplish a second development. In scores of texts—more than a hundred in all, of which about one-fourth had to do with the Roman Question—he reiterated that the essential claim which the Church makes on civil societies and their governments is stated in the ancient formula, "the freedom of the Church". It was not possible for him to complete these two developments with a third —the affirmation of the freedom of society and of the duty of governments toward the freedom of the people. In any event, his doctrinal work cleared the way for further progress in understanding the rightful secularity of society and State, as against the ancient sacral conceptions.

This progress reaches its inevitable term in the *Declaration on Religious Freedom*. The sacrality of society and State is now transcended as archaistic. Government is not *defensor fidei*. Its duty and rights do not extend to what had long been called *cura religionis,* a direct care of religion itself and of the unity of the Church within Christendom or the nation-state. The function of government is secular: that is, it is confined to a care of the free exercise of religion within society—a care therefore of the freedom of the Church and of the freedom of the human person in religious affairs. The function is secular because freedom in society, for all that it is most precious to religion and the Church, remains a secular value—the sort of value that government can protect and foster by the instrument of law. Moreover, to this conception of the State as secular, there corresponds a conception of society itself as secular. It is not only distinct from the Church in its origin and finality; it is also autonomous in its structures and processes. Its structural and dynamic principles are proper to itself and proper to the secular order—the truth about the human person, the justice due to the human person, the love that is the properly human bond among persons and, not least, the freedom that is the basic constituent and requirement of the dignity of the person.

This is the true Christian understanding of society and State in their genuine secularity which appears in *Pacem in terris*. The *Declaration on Religious Freedom* adds to it the final clarity in the essential detail, namely, that in the secular society, under the secular State, the highest value that both State and society are called upon to protect and foster is the personal and social value of the free exercise of religion. The values of religion itself for men and society are to be protected and fostered by the Church and by other religious communities availing themselves of their freedom. Thus the Declaration assumes its primary theological significance. Formally, it settles only the minor issue of religious freedom. In effect, it defines the Church's basic contemporary view of the world—of human society, of its order of human law and of the functions of the all too human powers that govern it. Therefore, the Declaration not only completes the *Decree on Ecumenism,* it also lays down the premise, and sets the focus, of the Church's concern with the secular world, which is the subject of Chapter XIII. Not nostalgic yearnings to restore ancient sacralizations, not futile efforts to find new forms of sacralizing the terrestrial and temporal order in its structures and processes, but the purification of these processes and structures and the sure direction of them to their inherently secular ends— this is the aim and object of the action of the Church in the world today.

In its own way, the Declaration is an act in that lengthy process known today as *consecratio mundi.* The document makes clear that the statute of religious freedom as a civil right is, in reality, a self-denying ordinance on the part of government. Secular government denies to itself the right to interfere with the free exercise of religion, unless an issue of civil offense against public order arises (in which case the State is acting only in the secular order, not in the order of religion). On the other hand, the ratification of the Declaration by Vatican Council II is, with equal clarity, a self-denying ordinance on the part of the Church. To put the matter simply and in historical perspective, the Church finally renounces, in principle, its long-cherished historical right to *auxilium brachii saecularis* (the phrase in Canon 2198 remains for the moment an odd bit of archaism). The secular arm is simply secular, inept for the furtherance of the proper purposes of the People of God. More exactly, the Church has no secular arm. In ratifying the principle of religious freedom, the Church accepts the full burden of the freedom which is the single claim she is entitled to make on the secular world. Thus a lengthy, twisting, often tortuous development of doctrine comes to a term.

Like all developments, this one will initiate a further progress in doctrine, that is, a new *impostazione* of the doctrine of the Church on the problem of Church and State, as it is called, in order to restore, and to perfect in its own sense, the authentic tradition. This, however, is a subject in itself, not to be dealt with here.

II

HISTORICAL CONSCIOUSNESS

The second great trend of the 19th century was the movement from classicism to historical consciousness. The meaning of these two terms would require lengthy explanation, both historical and philosophical. Suffice it to say here that classicism designates a view of truth which holds objective truth, precisely because it is objective, to exist "already out there now" (to use Bernard Lonergan's descriptive phrase). Therefore, it also exists apart from its possession by anyone. In addition, it exists apart from history, formulated in propositions that are verbally immutable. If there is to be talk of development of doctrine, it can only mean that the truth, remaining itself unchanged in its formulation, may find different applications in the contingent world of historical change. In contrast, historical consciousness, while holding fast to the nature of truth as objective, is concerned with the possession of truth, with man's affirmations of truth, with the understanding contained in these affirmations, with the conditions—both circumstantial and subjective—of understanding and affirmation, and therefore with the historicity of truth and with progress in the grasp and penetration of what is true.

The Church in the 19th century, and even in the 20th, opposed this movement toward historical consciousness. Here, too, the reason was obvious. The term of the historical movement was modernism, that "conglomeration of all heresies", as *Pascendi dominici gregis* called it. The insight into the historicity of truth and the insight into the role of the subject in the possession of truth were systematically exploited to produce almost every kind of pernicious "ism", unto the destruction of the notion of truth itself—its objective character, its universality, its absoluteness.

These systematizations were false, but the insights from which
they issued were valid. Here again a work of discernment needed
to be done, and was not done. To be quite summary about it,
this work had to wait until Vatican Council II. (I am not here
speaking of the work of scholars.)

The sessions of the Council have made it clear that, despite
resistance in certain quarters, classicism is giving way to historical
consciousness. Obviously, neither of these theories has been
debated, and perhaps they are not even understood as theories.
The significant thing is that the Council has chosen to call itself
"pastoral". The term has been misunderstood, as if the Council
were somehow not concerned with truth and doctrine but only
with life and practical directives for living. To so contrast the
pastoral and doctrinal would be disastrous. The pastoral concern
of the Council is a doctrinal concern. However, it is illuminated
by historical consciousness: that is, by concern for the truth not
simply as a proposition to be repeated but more importantly as
a possession to be lived; by concern, therefore, for the subject
to whom the truth is addressed; hence, also, by concern for the
historical moment in which the truth is proclaimed to the living
subject; and, consequently, by concern to seek that progress in
the understanding of the truth demanded both by the historical
moment and by the subject who must live in it. In a word, the
fundamental concern of the Council is with the development of
doctrine. The scholarly concern of the 20th century has become
also the pastoral concern of the Church in the 20th century.

Viewed in this light, the second theological significance of
the *Declaration on Religious Freedom* appears. The Declaration is a pastoral exercise in the development of doctrine. (This,
it may be said in passing, is why it met some opposition; classicism—if not as a theory, at least as an operative mentality—is
still with us, here and there.) Briefly, the Declaration bases itself
on a progress in doctrine that has, in fact, occurred since Leo
XIII. It also carries this progress one inevitable step further by
discarding an older theory of civil tolerance in favor of a new
doctrine of religious freedom more in harmony with the authen-

tic and more fully understood tradition of the Church. Only a bare outline of this progress can be suggested here.

The remote theological premise of the Declaration is the traditional teaching of the Church, clarified by Leo XIII, with regard to the two orders of human life, the sacred and the secular, the civil and the religious. The immediate premise is the philosophy of society and its juridical organization—in this sense, a philosophy of the State—developed by Pius XII and given a more systematic statement by John XXIII in *Pacem in terris*. This philosophy is deeply rooted in tradition; it is also, by comparison with Leo XIII, new.

The Leonine doctrine, more Aristotelian and medieval in inspiration, rested on the conception of the common good as an ensemble of social virtues and values, chiefly the value of obedience to the laws. The Pian and Joannine doctrine, more profoundly Christian in inspiration, rests on the conception of the common good as consisting chiefly in the effective exercise of the rights, and the faithful discharge of the duties, of the human person. Correlatively, in the Leonine conception the function of government was primarily ethical, namely, the direction of the citizen-subject—who was considered more subject than citizen— toward the life of virtue by the force of good laws reflecting the demands of the moral order. In the Pian and Joannine doctrine, on the other hand, the primary function of government is juridical, namely, the protection and promotion of the exercise of human and civil rights, and the facilitation of the discharge of human and civil duties by the citizen who is fully citizen, that is, not merely subject to, but also participant in, the processes of government.

The insight of Pius XII, which lay at the root of the new development, was stated thus: "Man as such, so far from being regarded as the object of social life or a passive element thereof, is rather to be considered its subject, foundation and end." In contrast, the customary focus of Leo XIII's doctrine was on the *principes* (his favorite word), the rulers who wielded in society the power they had received from God. In this latter conception, society is to be built and rendered virtuous from the top down, as it were; the role of government is dominant. In the former conception, however, society is to be built and rendered virtuous from the bottom up, as it were; the role of government is subordinate, a role of service to the human person. Moreover, in Leo XIII's conception (except in *Rerum novarum*), government was not only personal but paternal; the "prince" was *pater patriae,* as society was the family writ large. In Pius XII's conception, on the other hand, government is simply political; the relation between ruler and ruled is a civil relation, not familial. This was a return to tradition (notably to Aquinas), after the aberrations of continental absolutism and the exaggerations of the Roman-law jurists.

Leo XIII's paternal conception owed much to historical fact and to the political culture of his day. The pivotal fact was the *imperita multitudo,* the illiterate formless masses which reappear time and again in his text. In contrast, Pius XII's political conception was a return to tradition, to the noble idea of "the people", a structured concept at whose root stands, as he said, "the citizen [who] feels within himself the consciousness of his own personality, of his duties and rights, and of his due freedom as joined with a respect for the freedom and dignity of others". This return to the tradition of "the free man under a limited government" (as someone has summarized the basic political insight of Aquinas) was likewise a progress in the understanding of the tradition.

Finally, in Leo XIII the traditional distinction between society and State was largely lost from view; its disappearance from history had been, in fact, part of the *damnosa haereditas*—the fateful heritage—of the ancien régime. It is a noteworthy fact that nowhere in the immense body of Leo XIII's writings is there to be found a satisfactory philosophy of human law and jurisprudence. He was always the moralist, not the jurist. His concern was to insist that the juridical order of society must recognize the imperatives of the objective moral order. This emphasis was indeed necessary against the moral antinomianism and juridical positivism of continental laicism. However, in consequence of this polemic necessity, Leo XIII gave little if any attention to the internal structure of the juridical order itself—the structure, that is, of the State.

This became the preoccupation of Pius XII, as the menace of totalitarianism loomed large, threatening the basic dignity of the human person, which is his freedom. Pius XII revived the distinction between society and State, the essential barrier against totalitarianism. He also made it a pillar of his concept of the juridical State (the phrase is alien in English; we speak of "constitutional government"). The powers of government are not only limited to the terrestrial and temporal order. Since Leo XIII this had been clear doctrine, however much it may have been disregarded in practice. But even within this limited order, the powers of government are limited by the higher order of human rights, defined in detail in *Pacem in terris,* whose doctrine is completed by the *Declaration on Religious Freedom.* The safekeeping and promotion of these rights is government's first duty to the common good.

Even this rapid comparison may help to make clear that, although Leo XIII's theory of civil tolerance was coherent with his conception of society and State, it is not coherent with the more fully developed philosophy of Pius XII and John XXIII. For Leo XIII the power of the ruler was *patria potestas,* a paternal power. The ruler-father can, and is obliged to, know what is true and good—the true religion and the moral law. His primary duty, as father-ruler, is to guide his children-subjects— the illiterate masses—to what is true and good. His consequent function is to protect them against religious error and moral aberration—against the preachments of the "sects" (that favorite Leonine word). The masses are to be regarded as children, *ad instar puerorum,* who are helpless to protect themselves. They must look to the ruler-father, who knows what is true and good and also knows what is good for them. In these circumstances, and given this personal conception of rule, the attitude of government toward what is error and evil could only be one of tolerance. Government permits by law what it cannot prevent by law. Moreover, this civil tolerance is no more than a dictate of necessity; it is practiced for the sake of a greater good—the peace of the community. This theory of civil tolerance may indeed be regarded as a counsel of practical wisdom. It can hardly be regarded as permanent Catholic doctrine, any more than the theory of government, with which it is correlative, may be so regarded. The roots of both theories are in the contingencies of history, not in the exigencies of abiding truth.

Therefore, the *Declaration on Religious Freedom* puts aside the post-Reformation and 19th-century theory of civil tolerance. The fault is not error but archaism. A new philosophy of society and State has been elaborated, more transtemporal in its manner of conception and statement, less time-conditioned, more differentiated, a progress in the understanding of the tradition. Briefly, the structural elements of this philosophy are the four principles of social order stated, and developed in their exigencies, in *Pacem in terris*—the principles of truth, justice, love and freedom. The declaration of the human and civil right to the free exercise of religion is not only in harmony with, but also required by, these four principles. The foundation of the right is the truth of human dignity. The object of the right—freedom from coercion in religious matters—is the first debt due in justice to the human person. The final motive for respect of the right is a love of appreciation of the personal dignity of man. Religious freedom itself is the first of all freedoms in a well-organized society, without which no other human and civil freedoms can be safe.

Roland Bainton/*New Haven, Conn.*

Truth, Freedom and Tolerance: The View of a Protestant

The problem of religious liberty is vastly different for the Christian Churches in the 20th century from what it was in the 16th or even the 17th centuries. In the middle of the 16th century Pietro Carnesecchi, a former papal secretary, accused of deviations from orthodoxy, was condemned to be decapitated and burned in accord with a sentence pronounced by a conclave meeting in Rome under the presidency of Pope Pius V. A few years earlier in Protestant Geneva Michael Servetus, because of his denial of infant baptism and the Nicene formulation of the doctrine of the Trinity, was condemned by the town council to be burned at the stake in the name of the Father, the Son and the Holy Spirit. In our day the Protestants of Geneva have erected an expiatory monument to the memory of Servetus, and the Catholics, in the latest edition of the Canon Law by Cardinal Gasparri in 1911, have distinguished the provisions still in vogue from those now obsolete by printing the former as the text and the latter at the bottom of the pages. All of the corporal penalties for heresy have been consigned to the footnotes. The problem today for the Christian Churches centers on demands for: (1) freedom of public worship; (2) freedom for the public proclamation of one's faith; (3) freedom of education from compulsory instruction or exercises; (4) the complete neutrality of the State with respect to religious groups; (5) the public recognition of the validity of marriage, regardless of who performs it; (6) the absence of social discrimination against religious nonconformists to the prevailing pattern.

The change in attitude on the part of the Christian Churches may be attributed to a number of factors. One is the emergence of religious pluralism. Attempts at extermination of one group by another have failed, and the very attempts have so alienated many that they have left the Churches and added to the pattern those of no professed religion. Moreover the pluralism includes not only the Christian varieties, but also other religions. In many lands the Jews are a sizable minority, and the religions of the world have become neighbors to each other by reason of the increased speed of communication. Closer proximity has engendered respect, with the recognition that heretics, sectaries and infidels may be sincere, high-minded and noble. At the same time a closer study of the New Testament has brought home the realization, which should have been manifest centuries ago, that constraint of sincere conviction is incompatible with the mind of Christ.

Another factor affecting Christian attitudes is that the ideology which once led the Churches to persecute has been appropriated by anti-religious movements, marked by the fanaticism characteristic of Christian groups in the past and utilizing with technological refinements the methods once employed by the Inquisition to break the spirit of dissenters. At the same time rampant nationalism, conjoined with totalitarianism, has made a creed out of cruelty. Communism and fascism have sought to kill or cripple the Churches. Catholics and Protestants have become partners in suffering and their own differences have been dwarfed by confrontation with these monstrous perversions.

Quite possibly in reaction against the collectivism of communism and fascism, the Christian Churches are basing their claim for religious liberty upon the dignity of the person as an individual. This emphasis is comparatively new in Christianity. Until well into the 18th century the problem of religious liberty had to do with groups, and the territorial solution assigned particular localities to one or another religious body with no freedom for minorities or individual dissenters except through emigration. However, the demand today for liberty, even on the part of the religious groups, is based upon the inviolability of the consciences of its individual components.

In all likelihood a subsidiary reason why religious liberty is now deemed so precious is that other liberties are being curtailed even in those portions of the earth known as the "Free World". The sheer exigencies of the increase in population and the complexities of mechanization require more extensive controls. In the economic sphere government regulates production, prices, exports and imports. The United States is in the throes of decision whether to compel all labor to be unionized, in which case the worker will gain in wages and security at the price of freedom to deal individually with the employer. In the political domain the very number of the citizens precludes the town meeting on national problems, and more and more decisions involving the fate of millions rest with a very few heads of government. Circumscribed at so many points, man demands freedom to worship or not to worship God as he will, and governments in the "Free World" are more willing to concede this freedom because they see in it no threat to their own stability. Possibly the totalitarian powers pay the Churches a higher tribute by recognizing that they do stand in judgment upon all cultures, and the Churches of the "Free World" do well to ask themselves whether they are free because innocuous.

The theological ground for religious liberty in recent pronouncements, both Catholic and Protestant, is the dignity of man. One cannot but wonder why Christians should have taken so many centuries to perceive that the dignity of man precludes the enslavement of the body and the coercion of the spirit. Such retardation prompts one to inquire whence the dignity of man is derived and in what it consists. The answer given is that the dignity of man derives from his creation in the image of God. Here one must remember, however, that in Christian teaching man is believed to have fallen from his primal state, and the image of God in man is thought to have been obscured, though not obliterated. What then remains? Man's freedom of choice is the answer, for God does not constrain him. However, here we enter upon a very thorny subject. Although man is by common consent free to make choices, are those choices preconditioned by motives derived from circumstances beyond his control? Faith is described in Christian theology as a gift of God. But, since plainly all men do not receive the gift, are they then free?

We may be on sounder ground if we turn not to the beginning but rather to the end of man. Those in the Renaissance period who proclaimed the dignity of man—one thinks of Manetti and Pico—did so on an assumption, derived from a blend of Christian and Neoplatonic strains, that man is capable of union with God. As Irenaeus had said long since, God became man in order that man might become God. Man's dignity is thus centered not so much on man's creation as on God's incarnation in man and the possibility that, as divinity and humanity were conjoined in Christ, so man, rising above his animal nature, may be conjoined with God. The stress is not so much upon man's origin as upon his potential.

However, the process whereby man comes to be conjoined with God must be unconstrained by man. Slavish submission, resentful acquiescence, mechanical muttering of an incantation —these do not constitute union with God. There must indeed be submission, complete and unreserved, unconstrained by any external pressure. This union of man with God is strictly personal. It is as individual as death, and herein lies the dignity of man in Christian thinking.

If we are to achieve religious liberty throughout the world, we shall have to take more than Christians into account. They are a minority in the world at large, and genuine Christians are a minority in nominally Christian lands. What approach is to be made to the "men of goodwill" of whom Pope John spoke, the humanists, the atheists who cherish justice, humanity, mag-

nanimity and compassion? For them also there is a dignity of
man, as the Stoics affirmed long before the advent of Christ.
Man, they observed, is actually at the pinnacle of all sentient
beings, endowed with reason, with speech, with tears and laughter
whereby he is able to resolve his differences by converse rather
than compulsion. Because of his very constitution man should
be, as Seneca said, sacred to man. Being superior to the insensate
world, and threatened by it, all men in their common predicament
should rally to each other and not engage in mutual extermination.

When we come to deal with the totalitarians, the achievement
of a common premise for religious liberty is almost impossible.
They believe, to be sure, in the dignity of mankind, but not of
individual men, and they are willing to enslave and exterminate
millions for the sake of an ultimate society. Perhaps they are
not so different from those of the "Free World" who also will
pour out the blood of millions for the sake of national security.
However, there is a difference, inasmuch as with the totalitarians
individualism is crushed in collectivism. They may be told that
mankind cannot be served by liquidating men and that in the
end repression will prove futile, but there may be no way to
prove this to them other than by the blood of the martyrs.

Although one may indeed marvel that Christians should have
required some seventeen or eighteen centuries to perceive that
freedom of religion is a corollary of the dignity of man, the
reason is not difficult to discern. Constraint in religion was based
on truth and love. The welfare of man in this life and the next
was assumed to be dependent on membership in the Church,
participation in her sacraments and adherence to her creed—a
creed for which certainty was claimed. If, then, rejection of the
creed entailed damnation, love required that men be saved by
constraint from the consequences of their error, however sincerely
held.

Christians who call for religious liberty today do not absolutely
reject all of these assumptions. Truth is superior to error, and,
on the basis of truth and with the motive of love, sometimes

even religious beliefs may properly be subject to interference. An example is afforded by the experience of an American health officer at Manila some time ago. A report was brought to him that typhoid had broken out in various spots in the city. Investigation disclosed that a sewer had broken in the bay. The scum had assumed the shape of a cross. A native fisherman reported this as a miracle. The priest confirmed it and the populace went out in little boats, brought back some of the miraculous water and drank it. The health officer called out the militia and held back the people till the damage was repaired. This was a case of certainty with regard to truth, for the germ theory of disease has been confirmed by a century of clinical testing. No matter how sincerely the natives believed in the miracle, they were wrong and they were imperiling lives, their own and others. Surely it was a work of love to save them from their error.

However, religious knowledge can never claim such a high degree of certainty. The creed of the Church does not admit of clinical verification. The distinction between faith and knowledge is not to be obliterated. The most telling argument for persecution in the past has been that heresy would damn souls for all eternity, but the very assumption that conscious life will continue for all eternity is a matter of faith and not of demonstration. Therefore, the doctrine of immortality is a matter for private consolation rather than public legislation. At no point is there the degree of certainty in religion that warrants calling out the militia.

This is not to deny the concept of revelation. But what is revelation and how is it given? Protestants and Catholics alike are coming increasingly to recognize that revelation is not propositional. The Old Testament writer believed that God delivered the Ten Commandments to Moses engraved on tablets of stone. The apostle Paul asserted that the new dispensation was given not on tablets of stone, but upon hearts of flesh. God did not deliver a book; he became incarnate in a man who left nothing in writing and whose very sayings are recorded in variant forms. The revelation of God in Christ was the totality of an experience, meaningful only to those who yielded obedience, and not to most of those who beheld the Lord in the flesh, for he was rejected by men.

This revelation is not devoid of content and can be expressed in terms of concepts, but they are conditioned by the thought forms of each period in turn. The implications of the revelation experienced have been constantly subject to revision and reformulation. Christian theology moves between the poles of that which is given and that which is sought, between truth as a deposit and truth as a quest. This quest requires absolute sincerity on the part of the seeker. He who is sincere may not be right, but he who is insincere must of necessity be wrong. He who aspires to the truth can adhere to error only so long as he deems it to be truth. The way to persuade him to the contrary is not to shatter his integrity but to convince him of his mistake. The very nature of the quest is such that freedom is required—not only freedom to pursue the truth on one's own, but freedom to engage in discussion with others.

Truth is hammered out in the clash of minds. Almost invariably he who receives a new insight exaggerates, and his excessive claims must be moderated by others. The innovator needs the conservative to curb his exuberance and the conservative needs the innovator to shake his complacency. The optimism of Milton that truth always triumphs in free encounter may not be entirely warranted, for errors have persisted for centuries, but the assumption is not unwarranted that "truth crushed to earth will rise again". Moreover, even though the uninhibited interchange of minds may not always establish the truth, the repression of debate will certainly tend to perpetuate error.

The unconstrained clash of minds does not, however, issue in unanimity, let alone uniformity, but rather in variety. Then the difficult question arises as to whether the varieties are the different faces of a polygon or whether they are contraries and mutually exclusive. The answer depends on the evaluation of religious varieties. High Church and low, an elaborate liturgy and silent worship, the glory of the cathedral and the simplicity of the hermit's cell—are they all valid forms of religious expression? How much variety is possible within a structural unity? Should variety assume form in separate Churches, which by their competition stimulate each other in the quest for truth and in Christian endeavor? These questions are all very relevant with respect to the reunion of the Churches, but not so directly as regards religious liberty, except to illustrate how many perplexing problems there are which no constraint can ever solve. There must be fluidity, searching of soul and matching of minds in love and with respect.

In the practical realm, by common consent there are certain limits to religious liberty. In recent discussions of the subject one frequently encounters the expression "with due limits". But what are they? All agree that freedom does not include liberty to interfere with the liberty of another. A second principle, sometimes mentioned, is that religious liberty must not disturb the public peace. The formula will have different meanings depending on what does disturb the public peace. We all today repudiate the territorial solution of religious pluralism whereby each region has its own religion and minorities have freedom only to emigrate, but if people of different faiths will not live side by side without cutting each other's throats, what can be done if not to separate them? This appears to be the situation in Pakistan and India, between Moslems and Hindus. However, although in such a case State intervention may be necessary, grave care should be exercised that it not be invoked simply to maintain the status quo. Suppose civil rights demonstrators, white and black, are praying on a sidewalk in front of a segregated church at the hour of worship. A deacon of the church orders them away on the ground that they are disturbing public worship. Whose worship is being disturbed? The question is one for the courts to answer, but let not intervention be weighted on the side of the prevailing mores.

By mentioning this case we are already trenching upon practical issues which must engage us. The thorniest in those lands where the State is not hostile to religion center on the relations of Church and State. The age-old solution has been the division of spheres variously described as the two kingdoms, or the two swords, and contrasted as secular and sacred, temporal and eternal, physical and spiritual. However, since man himself is not bifurcated, the spheres necessarily overlap, and doubly so because the Church, as a property-holding corporation, is involved in the temporal order, and because the State regards religious attitudes as essential to the well-being of the commonwealth. In many lands and for many centuries the Orthodox Churches in the East and the Catholic Church in the West, together with the more recent Protestant national Churches, have been established. This system, if dissenters are persecuted, is intolerable. If they are subject to no civil or educational disabilities, the situation is still undesirable. The established Church may suffer from State interference, as in England where a Baptist prime minister has been known to appoint an Anglican bishop and the revision of the prayer book to depend on Parliament. From the standpoint of the sects there is still a measure of social discrimination because membership in the establishment carries with it prestige. From the standpoint of the nation the situation is undesirable because there is danger of hypocrisy when only a fraction of the population takes the established Church seriously. The estimate has been made that in Sweden with an establishment there is less popular enthusiasm for Christianity than in Russia under persecution.

Where Church and State are separate and religion has assumed multiple forms, the State is required to be neutral, giving no special favor to any. But may it then give favor to all without distinction? The difficulty here is that the pluralism includes those whose religion consists in having no religion. The atheists demand that the State be divested of all religious functions and expressions. They may be few, but the principle of religious liberty requires that the minority always win. In recent years the United States Supreme Court has rendered a number of decisions designed to maintain the absoluteness of the wall of separation between Church and State. One wonders whether the distinction is not being made too absolute. That the State should not prescribe and require a fixed form of prayer in the public schools is an obvious corollary from the principle of separation, but does it follow that no form should ever be allowed? If the purpose is to avoid an affront to the conscience of a minority, what happens if there is no minority? In certain sections of Pennsylvania, for example, the public schools have only the children of the Amish. In such a case prayer can be a sincere religious exercise offensive to none. This example suggests that the problem might be handled on a regional rather than a national basis.

State aid to parochial schools in the form of bus transportation, free lunches and textbooks is defended by some on humanitarian grounds and attacked by others as prying the mortar out of the wall of separation. This is precisely the point at which the separation is most difficult to define and maintain. The pot in which the melting of the peoples has taken place in the United States is the public school. Here the children of all races and creeds, and, increasingly, of all colors, are intimately associated from the earliest years. The State cannot but view with dismay the possible disintegration of the public school. The Churches, on the other hand, cannot view with complacency the exclusion of all religious instruction from the regular hours of schooling except insofar as the religions of the world are described as items of information and Christianity is given no preference over the religion of the Aztecs. There appears to be no way out, save by some sort of a compromise or, shall we say, adjustment. Various attempts have been made and are being made in the United States and elsewhere to do justice to the claims both of the State and of the Churches in the field of education. The solution will have to be found in the crucible of experience rather than by the application of rigid principles.

Again there are those who demand that the State should give no favor to religious bodies in the form of exemption from taxation. But is this exemption granted to Churches because they are religious bodies as such or because they are non-profit organizations contributing to the public welfare on a par with museums, libraries, schools and social settlements? The fact that the Churches are at the same time religious ought not to disqualify them. Whether their internal freedom is jeopardized by reason of such favor is for them to decide.

Should there be chaplains in the army and the halls of Congress, in uniform and paid by the government? Preferably not. They will be better able to render a spiritual ministry if they are free from any State control. Let them be supported by the Churches and garbed in whatever dress a particular Church deems appropriate. Should the government proclaim any religious holidays such as Thanksgiving? If the proclamation employs the language of religion, the atheists will object. However, there is no reason why the State should not fix holidays which may coincide with religious observances. Should there be prayer at the opening of Congress and the inauguration of the president? If there is objection, the answer may be to observe a period of silence. Even an atheist can scarcely be outraged by a solemn hush.

Now we come to the problem of how far the separation of Church and State restricts the freedom of the Church. The experience of the centuries has taught us to fear a clerical theocracy. At the same time the Church does seek to permeate society with Christian ideals, and she is very much concerned that the State should implement justice and humanity together with all the civil virtues. Luther's formula was that the minister should be the mentor of the magistrate. But then comes the difficulty that the ministers of different Churches give contrary advice, and even the members of a single congregation are not of one mind with regard to particular courses of political action. However, this does not mean that in consequence the ministers and the Churches must restrict themselves to purely spiritual concerns, or even that they must refrain from lobbying, in the sense of sending delegations to influence legislators. In all such activities, however, the Churches are not so much Churches as societies or individuals, along with other societies and persons, eager to promote particular social objectives rather than to conduct particular modes of worship. In this area the Churches are no more privileged and no more restricted than the labor unions.

May the Churches and individual Christians go so far as not merely to try to influence the government but even to refuse to obey the government? The Church has never forsaken the dictum that God is to be obeyed rather than man. But since what man commands is relatively clear and what God demands in particular instances is far from being obvious, the decision as to what constitutes the will of God rests with individuals singly or in groups. Consequently the clash with the State centers sometimes on the opposition of Churches but more commonly in our own day on conscientious objection and civil disobedience as practiced by individuals.

At this point a distinction needs to be made between degrees of disobedience. In the United States, where a law must be constitutional in order to be binding, the only way to find out whether it is constitutional is to disobey it and thereby create a test case. Properly speaking, the term disobedience does not apply until after the Supreme Court has rendered a decision. But even the Supreme Court is not necessarily right, or better, the Constitution is not necessarily right. The Fugitive Slave Law was not unconstitutional. Yet some of the Churches deemed it to be wrong and refused obedience. For the Christian the law of the State must yield to a higher law, whether it be called the law of nature or the law of God.

Yet he who disobeys the laws of States must expect to incur some penalty, since the State cannot maintain its structure if it allows its laws to be set aside at the discretion of individuals. The State should aim, however, at nothing more than the observance of the law. The purpose of penalty is not to break down the integrity of the objector. The State must not forget that he who goes to prison for conscientious objection to a particular requirement, after the case has ceased to be relevant and he is released, may be on other counts a most devoted servant of the State. In

England, for example, men who have been penalized for opposition to particular wars, have later been prime ministers.

Religious liberty applies also within the structure of the Church. How far shall she discipline her own members? A voluntary society can scarcely exist if it does not have a set of principles, objectives and standards that members are required to accept and exemplify. There are Protestants who have a phobia against any sort of heresy trial, yet would not think it improper for a secular society to read a member out of the party. In practice the Church needs to find a middle way between disintegrating latitude and stultifying rigidity. And this requires a distinction between essentials to be required and non-essentials to be left optional. Room for variety must be allowed if the Church is to escape stagnation; great consideration should be given to a disquieting member who himself believes that he is in essential agreement with the Church and is seeking to reform rather than to destroy. With regard to moral offenders the Church cannot abrogate all disciples, but protracted exclusion from the sacraments and fellowship of the Church may harden and alienate rather than reclaim the wrongdoer. Above all, the censures of the Church must not automatically coincide with the penalties of the State. If a conscientious objector to war refuses any form of alternate service and goes to prison, he should remain a member of the Church and should receive every measure of encouragement to be faithful to his own conscientious conviction, even though it is not shared by the majority of his fellow Church members. And if a minister goes to prison rather than pay taxes which are expended mainly for military purposes, he is not to be deposed from his ministry. The State will have to penalize, but the Church should uphold.

The principle of religious liberty calls for a spirit of moderation, respect and persuasion rather than coercion.

C. Jaime Snoek, C.SS.R./*Juiz de Fora, Brazil*

The Third World, Revolution and Christianity

Mankind is gradually becoming aware of the dramatic situation of the so-called Third World, increasingly alienated, increasingly angry but also increasingly determined to take its place among the nations of the world, to assume its proper historical role. Lebret's great achievement, with his harnessing of economics with humanism, demonstrated to the West, by means of incontrovertible research and statistics, the Third World's tragedy and has shown it the precariousness of its suicidal policies.[1] His prophetic preaching was not without effect. The Church took a firm stand, especially in *Mater et Magistra,* in *Pacem in terris* and in Paul VI's historic speech at the United Nations. R. Coste's recent "Morale Internationale" places great emphasis on the matter, referring to it in Lebret's words as "the drama of the century".[2]

What is the situation of this Third World? Lebret describes it as a vicious circle of poverty, with excessively unfavorable chances with regard to life expectancy (in northeast Brazil infant mortality exceeds 50% and the average man can barely look forward to thirty years of life), with regard to illness (at worst,

[1] L.-J. Lebret, *Suicide ou survie de l'Occident* (Paris, 1958); *idem, O drama do século XX* (São Paulo, 1962).
[2] R. Coste, *Morale Internationale (Bibliothèque de Théologie. Théologie morale,* Série II, Vol. 10, Paris, 1964), p. 465.

one doctor per 71,000 people), with regard to hunger (the rich peoples eat four times more food than the poor ones). Unless the rich countries change their course radically and move rapidly toward a solidary civilization, the backwardness of the poor countries will become ever more acute and distressing. These countries' increasing awareness of their poverty, of others' plenty and of their own potential strength has created a climate of revolt, greatly vulnerable to the Marxist education that produced the "miracle" of social revolution in Russia, China and Cuba. The recent crises in the Congo, in Vietnam and in the Dominican Republic reaffirm that a solution to the problem of underdevelopment is vital to the building of a new world of universal peace.

REVOLUTIONARY FERMENT IN LATIN AMERICA

In this article we can focus our attention only on some aspects of such a vast problem. One great restriction immediately imposes itself. It is not possible to refer to the Third World as one whole without falling into excessively vague generalizations. For this reason we shall concentrate our attention more on Latin America without, however, losing sight of the remaining underdeveloped countries. This restriction is justifiable. The Latin American nations undeniably constitute a certain historico-cultural unit and cannot be compared casually with the Afro-Asian nations. The gunshot which in 1775 began the American War of Independence and started the first great revolutionary wave of national emancipation, was heard quite soon in Latin America, even earlier than in various parts of Europe. Nevertheless, once independence had been won, it was not the progressives but the feudal classes that took power. They reaffirmed the colonial order and paid little attention to technical and industrial advance. National development stagnated and did not reach the whole of the people. In the serene possession of their own territory, tongue and culture, the Latin American nations spent the disturbed 19th century in a state of inertia and isolation. Their participation in international trade was from an advantageous position, due to the high prices of the products they exported and the still insignificant development of the industrial products they had to buy. All this changed suddenly after the Second World War. Backward for more than a century, Latin America was thrust into the very middle of the technical age, at the same time experiencing a demographic explosion, an awakening of the masses, flight from the countryside and the formation of large urban agglomerations peopled with poor ex-peasants, helpless and living at bare survival level. The rural sector, unproductive because of inadequate organization, is being increasingly neglected. The service sector is increasing out of all proportion. A feeble middle class feels itself squeezed between the traditional governing class and the masses seeking integration in the life of the nation. These serious internal tensions are aggravated by the fact of Latin America having fallen under the influence of international economic imperialism. The invasion by foreign firms, in reality consumers of capital, prevents the creation of native enterprises. The distance between the rich and the poor, between the developed countries and Latin America becomes increasingly more difficult to bridge. The realization of this situation (unavoidable with modern means of communication) produced a pre-revolutionary climate and led Latin America to consider itself involved in what Toynbee calls the third revolutionary wave, the revolution of the Third World.[3] It thus became aware of being, with the Bandung Conference Nations, the bone of contention between the two poles of domination.

Thus Latin America has much affinity with the Third World but at the same time represents a quite distinct section due to its

[3] A. Toynbee, *America and the World Revolution* (London and New York: Oxford University Press, 1962), p. 8. J. Comblin, *Nação e Nacionalismo* (São Paulo, 1965), pp. 134ff.; *Situação social da América Latina* (Centro Latino-Americano de Pesquisas em Ciências Sociais, Rio de Janeiro, 1965); "Revolución en América Latina," in *Mensaje* 115 ([3]1963); "Reformas revolucionárias en América Latina," in *Mensaje* 123 (1963); C. Furtado, *A pré-revolução brasileira* (Rio de Janeiro, [2]1962); C. Mendes de Almeida, *Nacionalismo e desenvolvimento* (Rio de Janeiro, 1963); F. Houtart, "Servicio Social y Transformación Social en América Latina," in *Service Social dans le Monde* 21 (1962), pp. 122-29.

deep Christian imprint. Therefore, within this context there appears the opportunity for a dialogue of Christianity with the body of problems posed by development, a dialogue which will only be genuine to the extent of its radicalism; that is, while it really is a confrontation stripped of any pretense of triumphing or of isolation in a new form of "Christianity". The Christian element in Latin America must be taken into a new dimension of criticism and, in a certain sense, of subjection. How will this confrontation come about? This is the problem that merits closer study.

Development, in the historical sense of complete integration of the marginal masses into the life of a nation and of the underdeveloped countries into the community of nations, is not possible without rapid and profound reform of the social order, without the so-called social revolution. This is the conviction held by large sections of the Latin American people, most of all by a notable group of intellectuals. It is impressive to note how the idea of social revolution has spread fast even among Christians. Strong impetus was given, without doubt, by the Chilean periodical *Mensaje* which, in two special issues, weighty in their content and brave in their stand, clearly opted for revolution in Latin America.[4] It is a rich source which will be amply used in this study. It was followed by numerous publications which refer to the essential and urgent necessity of this revolution.[5] Christians from various parts of Latin America have already chosen it and are now living a life of involvement in which they have accepted its risks in the hope of playing an active and reforming part in the crucial times in which they live. There is in existence in Latin America a trade union movement of personal Christian inspiration (CLASC), describing itself as being explicitly revolutionary and with increasing influence, especially among the peasants. In other words, we are even now faced with an already active move-

[4] Cf. footnote 3.
[5] Among others: J. Pinto de Oliveira, *Evangelho e revolução social* (São Paulo, 1962); L. Dewart, *Christianity and Revolution: The Lesson of Cuba* (New York, 1963); F. Houtart, E. Pin, "L'Eglise à l'heure de l'Amérique Latine," in *Eglise Vivante* (Tournai, 1965), pp. 94ff.; P.-E. Charbonneau, *Cristianismo, Sociedade e Revolução* (São Paulo, 1965).

ment demanding recognition. Neutrality is no longer possible. The word revolution is ambiguous. It evokes the violent revolutions of Russia, China and Cuba. Some think that Christians should eschew its use.[6] This, however, seems unrealistic to us. Nobody owns a word. This one has become popularized. It is better to define its import with accuracy. Here unanimity has been reached in practice. By revolution is understood a deliberately produced, rapid and profound change that affects all the basic systems (political, judicial, social and economic) and that is related to an ideology and a plan. It differs from evolution through the speed and purposiveness of the process. Thus conceived it has nothing to do with the *putsch* or with the *coup*. It implies, in its proper meaning, an element of rupture with the current social order and the building of a new order. Insurrection and violence may accompany the revolutionary movement but are not essential to it.[7]

DEVELOPMENT AND REVOLUTION WITHIN A THEOLOGICAL PERSPECTIVE

We start, therefore, from this global concept and ask: Has Christianity any contribution to make to this revolutionary process? In theology little thought has been given to revolution. This can be explained. Churches, even those born of the Reformation, have always allied themselves to the traditional social order and to power, with the exception of Calvinism.[8] "Never has a Church been seen to side with a revolution for the simple reason of its

[6] B. de Margerie, "Pode o Católico de 1963 dizer-se Néo-capitalista, Revolucionário ou Socialista?" in *Rev. Ecl. Bras.* 23 (1963), pp. 687ff.; G. Jarlot, "Riforme o revoluzione nell'America Latina," in *Civ. Catt.* 115 ([2]1964), p. 358.

[7] Glossary, *Mensaje* 115 (1963), p. 13; J. Comblin, *Nação e Nacionalismo* (São Paulo, 1965), p. 150; F. Houtart, "Sur le concept de révolution," in *Esprit* 33 (1965) n. 340, pp. 45-52; R. Coste, *Morale Internationale,* p. 409; Charbonneau, *op. cit.,* p. 70; R. Arias Calderón, "La universidad en la revolución latinoamericana," in *Presente* 3 (1965), pp. 20-35; P. González Loyola, "La révolution: une chose concrète et positive," in *Labor* 38 (1965), pp. 131-37.

[8] J. Comblin, *Théologie de la paix* II (Paris, 1963), pp. 114ff.

being just," wrote Merleau-Ponty in a biting criticism.[9] Prisoner as it was of a cosmocentric vision of reality, an ecstatic vision of a supposedly divine and immutable order, it could hardly be otherwise. It is only in the last decades that in actual philosophic and theological thinking there has occurred a profound revolution that appears to make possible the elaboration of a theology of development and revolution. Its first fruits are beginning to appear.[10] Here we can outline only some of its principles.

The anthropocentric view of the cosmos, the evolutionary concept of the universe and the awareness of history appear to be fundamental to modern thought.[11] Into this framework, which in essence is biblical, concepts such as development and revolution can easily be fitted. Nor is it possible to conceive of a status quo of a "sacred" and untouchable order if the biblical message reveals to us an immense divine movement, a movement of increasing humanization of man and of the progressive gathering together of all nations into one whole, starting with the creation and going on until the eschatological consummation. It is just that faith in an absolute and transcendental future, in a profound transfiguration which will be realized at the end of time with the coming of the Lord, which gives to all human endeavors an *élan* and a dynamism toward this goal, and, at the same time, a relative and temporary character. How can the Christian therefore find alien the transitoriness of human systems? How can he find revolutionary processes foreign to him, and, on principle, stand aside, if God himself revolutionized history through the incarnation of the Logos, through the splendor of the paschal mystery, through the Church of the Word incarnate, through the sanctifying Spirit who renews all and, by means of earthly realities, leads toward the full realization of his kingdom? [12] Christianity is the

[9] Mentioned by Comblin, *op. cit.*, I, p. 84.

[10] Among Catholics the pioneer was E. Mounier. Of the Protestants we mention P. Lehmann and R. Shaull.

[11] H. de Lima Vaz, *Cristianismo e consciencia histórica* (São Paulo, 1963).

[12] K. Rahner, "L'Avenir chrétien de l'homme," in *Inform. Cath. Intern.* 242 (1965), pp. 3ff.; *idem,* "A caminho do 'homem novo'," in *Igreja*

religion of the "coming to be", of the active expectation of the future. It is also the religion of development. When God deigned to become man the astounding possibility of human divinization was revealed to us. In Christ "it hath well pleased the Father that all fullness should dwell" (Col. 1, 19); that is the supreme realization of the possibilities of the human nature.[13] He is the distant goal toward which all development will proceed "until we meet . . . unto a perfect man, unto the measure of the age of the fullness of Christ" (Eph. 4, 13). In him also there began the effective and irresistible gathering together of all nations toward the messianic peace in unity (Matt. 8, 11; Apoc. 21, 24-26).

In concrete terms, God acts through the agency of mankind and within human history. It is because of this that God's same saving and humanizing love, which found its final expression in Christ, also forms the essence of Christianity. This love, universal and personal, will not rest while the other does not achieve its human completeness, while it does not participate in the universal community of love. It does not reconcile itself with dehumanizing social systems, with situations that represent the domination of one man over another, of one nation over another. It acts as a ferment, it exerts pressure. In this way, to sum up, Christianity, explicit or implicit, is the most intimately creative source of all radical changes in man's condition on earth while they represent an advance (or at least a striving toward greater love and freedom, toward greater brotherhood, toward greater humanity). The ideals of freedom and justice, which, although distorted, inspired the revolutions of 1789 and 1917, are Christian ideas born on Christian ground as P. Bigo says.[14] Since all humanity derives

---

hoje 7 (Petrópolis, 1964) ("Unterwegs zum 'neuen Menschen'," in *Wort und Wahrheit* [1961], pp. 807ff.); F. Houtart, "L'Eglise et le monde," in *L'Eglise aux cent visages* 12 (Paris, 1964), pp. 87ff.; P. Lehmann, *Ethics in a Christian Context* (New York, 1963).

[13] K. Rahner, "Anthropologie," in *Lex. Theol. u. Kirche* I (1957), pp. 618-27.

[14] P. Bigo, "Cristianismo y revolución en la época contemporánea," in *Mensaje* 115, p. 21.

from Christ, development is impossible to envisage without Christianity in one form or another.

Development, as we understand it, is therefore the actual saving, humanizing action of God, but embedded in the history of mankind. It is the same providence of God which the Bible describes as the work of him who gives justice to the poor and scatters the proud, who puts down the mighty from their seat and exalts the humble (Luke 1, 51-53). But this providence is executed by men, by human history, in whose midst the People of God live as a sacrament of that presence, as the community of God interacting continuously with the community of men, constituting the only history of salvation. Inseparable from, but at the same time transcending this history, God judges, saves, condemns, restores, destroys so as better to build his kingdom of justice and love, ever writing straight on man's crooked lines, ever guaranteeing the eventual success of his work. It is through his people, through those who belong to him visibly or invisibly, consciously or unconsciously, that God leads to the development and salvation of nations.[15] Looked at from this point of view there can be no doubt that the Christian's place is in the front line, at the heart of every genuine movement for human betterment.

By this we do not wish to assert that it will always be very obvious where and how the Christian should involve himself. Since sin became a part of history, this advance toward development became sinuous and convulsive, full of ambiguities. There are retreats and periods of stagnation, instabilities and reversals. What is relative and transitory is idolized. What is uncertain is considered absolute. Selfishness creates or preserves institutions of domination. At the very heart of history there is the cross of Christ, sign of conflict and of salvation. By means of all these trials, God purifies and saves, reveals the mystery of iniquity and of institutionalized sin which he judges, and leads gently but firmly toward the transcendental end of history. Only he who has faith and lives in the center of these conflicting situations sees in them something that discloses God's design.

[15] J. Comblin, *Théologie de la paix* I (Paris, 1960), pp. 95-142.

Bearer and instrument of peace, heir to the messianic promises, the People of God do not believe in holy wars.[16] They abhor violence (Matt. 5, 38-41). Wars and violent revolutions show that the influence of God's kingdom is still small. Relying on these promises, Christians would rather believe in the increasing possibility of preventing conflicts and the primitive violence they entail. While always seeking peaceful solutions, they do not cower behind the pretext of pacifism. When involved in unavoidable violent conflicts, they will still remain an element of reconciliation, of *rapprochement* between groups that are distressingly separated and opposed.

Concrete Responsibilities

Within this general review we now wish to suggest some specific courses of action. Let us examine the role of the Church (1), of involved Christians (2), of the ruling class (3) and of developed countries (4) with regard to the revolution of the Third World.

1. *The Church's Role*[17]

The Church's mission in the midst of the starving and oppressed must have its own character. It cannot flee from the problem of poverty. In other words, Christianization and humanization spring from the same evangelical inspiration.[18] Christianization includes humanization. But to turn humanization into Christianization, an awareness through faith of the former's relation to Christ is needed. Therefore the Church should be completely at one with the mankind it wishes to save, in a love made effective through its practice and planning, preparing and expressing the community of faith and of worship.

To the hierarchy itself there belongs above all the great pastoral

---

[16] *Ibid.*, p. 73.

[17] Cf. Houtart-Pin, *L'Eglise à l'heure de l'Amérique Latine,* pp. 198-223; M. Zañartu, "Religión y desarollo," in *Mensaje* 123, pp. 645ff.; J. Meert, "A Igreja face à Revolução Social no Terceiro Mundo," in *Rev. Conf. Relig. Brasil* 11 (1965), pp. 483ff.

[18] D. Helder Câmara, "Evangelização e Humanização num mondo em desenvolvimento," in *Rev. Ecl. Brasil* 25 (1965), p. 269.

instrument of the prophetic Word (Jer. 22, 13-19; Luke 6, 24-26;
James 5). Its silence will be interpreted as complicity. In the
practice of the great social teachings of the ministry, the hierarchy
should illuminate consciences with the light of the Gospel and, in
the midst of the obscurity of ambiguous situations, should open
a Christian perspective for the militant. It can be asked whether
the clergy in Latin America is sufficiently disengaged from unjust
systems.[19] It can be asked whether the missionaries of the various
Churches in Latin America do not, at times, without knowing,
let themselves be used as instruments of subtle neo-colonialism,
as in the past.[20] In spite of these doubts, an awakening in the
hierarchy can easily be perceived. Various episcopates and many
bishops have gone so far as to make brave and incisive pronouncements, tracing out clear plans for action along the lines of basic
reform.[21] All that could be desired is greater unity, greater uniformity in the pronouncements. The differences among the clergy
and, above all, in the episcopate leave laymen perplexed and
cripple their activity. There is also the need for greater integration with the Protestant Churches which are developing highly
intensive modes of social action starting from identical points
of view.[22] It would be one of the forms of ecumenism recommended by the *Decree on Ecumenism* (n. 12) of Vatican Council II, perhaps the most applicable to Latin America.

Although the Word may be the instrument most specific to
the Church in her self-fulfillment, as we have already said, she
will have to give a more concrete testimony of her love for men.
Without concrete action she will not be heard above the storm.
One most important task is hers by right: education of man, at

[19] See the impressive testimony of a Colombian trade union leader in a
letter to the pope in the review *Vozes* 59 (1965), pp. 698ff.

[20] R. Delavignette, *Christianisme et Colonialisme* (Paris, 1960), p. 55.

[21] The pastoral letter of 1962 of the Chilean episcopate and the 1963
message of the central committee of the Brazilian episcopate merit
especial prominence. For these and other documents see Houtart-Pin,
op. cit., footnote 17, pp. 211ff.

[22] *Ibid.*, p. 223. As early as 1953 Rev. R. Schaull published *O Cristianismo e la Revolução Social* (São Paulo). The World Council of Churches
has organized in recent years two seminars on Christianity and social
revolution in Latin America.

all levels and in all its ramifications. This does not mean that she should own a network of Catholic schools, colleges and universities. In many cases these have a negative value because of their mediocrity, because of the racial and social discrimination which is in force in them. But whatever the instrument, may she fulfill this task, this diaconate of educating (*e-ducere!*) the whole human potential, all the truly human values disinterestedly, without falling into the temptation of imposing Christianity, of clerical domination.

2. *The Laymen Involved in the Revolutionary Process*

The revolution in which all Christians can and should be involved, in the measure in which the current systems are unjust and incapable of adaptation, presupposes, by definition, a general idea of the new order one would like to see established. Pure and simple subversion or a revolution that does no more than redistribute wealth would be worse than the status quo in spite of its injustices. "The world of today has greater need for sages than planners," writes Lebret.[23] Without a clear philosophy and an ethic of development that can attract an already awakened people, Christians will not be able to counter the fascination of Marxism or the seduction of neo-capitalism—which both originate abroad. Therefore Latin America would lose a historic opportunity of moving toward its own solution of its problems with an effective Christian participation and thus to contribute in an original manner to the enhancement of the whole human family. The central idea will have to be a development for the benefit of mankind: the integral fulfillment of the whole man and of all men. The guidelines for a solidary civilization (with its community of interests) are being drawn but there still remains much to be done.[24]

[23] L.-J. Lebret, "Pour une éthique du développement," in *Economie et Humanisme* 22 (1963), p. 10.
[24] *Ibid.*, *Manifesto por uma civilização solidária* (São Paulo, 1961) (*Manifeste pour une civilization solidaire*, 1959); J.-Y. Calvez, "El cristiano frente al desarollo," in *Mensaje* 115, pp. 128ff.; R. Coste, "Morale Internationale," p. 526.

Nevertheless, a Christian conscience really immersed in the problems of a social revolution and committed to it cannot remain on the level of principles alone. It will be necessary to elaborate a concrete ethic, based on an objective analysis of the facts and aiming at concrete projects for basic reform, integrated into a global plan. One noteworthy attempt in this direction for Latin America was made by the staff of *Mensaje*.[25] There is the further need to create the agencies essential to carrying out the reforms so planned. Given the hypertrophy of the body politic, quite general in Latin America, it will be much more important to set up basic organizations (*e.g.*, for adult education) and intermediate bodies (trade unions, cooperatives, friendly or mutual aid societies) than political instruments. At the same time they will insure against the danger of technocracy.[26] It is the path pointed out by John XXIII in *Mater et Magistra* with regard to the peasants. It is the only sound path since it acts in depth. *A priori* it does not appear advisable to organize these intermediate bodies on a religious basis.

Faced with the radicalization of the revolutionary process, the Christian should not rely only on that which is relative and transitory in this radicalization but should bring his own principles to bear in making explicit the underlying values. The question of violence or non-violence falls into this perspective. A calling for human recognition and a susceptibility to absolute appeals give the Christian a definite preference for positive non-violence.[27] He does not allow himself to be carried away by revolutionary impatience.[28] Nevertheless, at the present phase of civilization we cannot yet exclude *a priori* the legitimacy of temporary recourse to illegality and violence. It is necessary to remember that, in a

---

[25] *Mensaje* 123; cf. L.-J. Lebret, *Dynamique concrète du développement* (Paris, 1961); G. Myrdal, *Beyond the Welfare State* (London: Duckworth, 1960).

[26] R. Venegas, "Organizaciones de base y cuerpos intermedios," in *Mensaje* 123, pp. 627ff.

[27] R. Coste, "Pacifism and Legitimate Defense," in *Concilium* 5 (1965), pp. 80ff.; F. Lepargneur, "Introdução a uma Teologia da Não-Violencia evangélica," in *Rev. Ecl. Brasil.* 25 (1965), pp. 220-43.

[28] Pius XII quoted in *Mensaje* 115, p. 91; *Pacem in terris* (n. 161).

certain sense, violence is already being used by the "counter-revolution", which persecutes union leaders (and not only Marxist ones!) and, being the privileged beneficiary of the status quo, has seen itself unable to fight the poverty that daily claims its victims. It is the violence exercised discreetly and silently by general hunger. According to a recognized moral principle, all reverts to the community in situations of extreme necessity. Is this principle not applicable here? And how can this be put into practice without some recourse to violence? Would not the dangers of personal possession be greater than those of revolutionary impatience?

In either case, the decision will be extremely delicate. The little that can be said regarding the conditions that might justify recourse to violence in such varied revolutionary situations has been derived from doctrinal tradition in well-known arguments which we need not reproduce.[29] Violence will be the last recourse in the face of a system essentially unjust and unbearable, and only upon the condition that there is sufficient certainty that a just system may be established within a short period. H. Thielicke demands that the new governing body be already potentially constituted, that the right moment in history be awaited and that there be ratification of the whole situation on the part of the people.[30] Obviously the choice of ways and methods must follow vigorously the demands of human dignity.[31] The revolutionaries must resist the double temptation of perpetuating their position in power, thus creating a new form of tyranny, and of thinking that this revolution is going to set up paradise for all time. In the distressing situations where Christians fight with arms, may they always be ready to reopen the dialogue.

Up to now we have taken as starting point the premise of a violent revolution waged by Christians. Much more delicate is

[29] Cf. J. Aldunate, "El deber moral ante la situación revolucionária," in *Mensaje* 115, pp. 87ff.; G. Claps, "El cristiano frente a la revolución violenta," *ibid.*, pp. 138ff.; W. Schollgen, *Aktuelle Moralprobleme* (Düsseldorf, 1955), pp. 240ff.; A. de Soras, "Insurrection," in *Catholicisme Hier, Aujourd'hui, Demain* 22 (1962), pp. 1815ff.

[30] Thielicke, *Theologische Ethik* II, II. Teil (Tubingen, 1958), pp. 425ff.

[31] R. Coste, *op. cit.*, pp. 339-420.

the taking of sides by Christians faced with a movement of Marxist inspiration. J. Terra carried out an excellent analysis of three different situations, corresponding to real historical situations: (1) the Marxist revolution that may yet have worthy intentions; (2) the definitely Marxist revolution that may, however, be defeated; (3) the irresistible Marxist revolution. For the details we refer to this author.[32]

3. The Ruling Class

It was, without doubt, liberal capitalism which gave the first push toward economic development in Latin America. We do not want to deny it this praise. But it is no less true that it is most to blame for the profound social irregularities of the present time.[33] The serious accusations of *Quadragesimo anno* against the abuse of economic power are still completely valid against the oligarchies of various Latin American countries. They hold the reins of power and the instruments of coercion. They also own powerful means of social communication, profoundly influencing public opinion. They suppress each attempt at social reform with the excuse of fighting communism. A certain group, called by Toynbee the Herodians, goes so far as to suppress its whole native way of thought and to live in the manner of the high society of the rich countries, depositing its money in European and North-American banks, making expensive trips abroad and becoming increasingly remote from its people.[34] It is alarming to note how the ruling class isolates itself from the Church's social teaching, often corrupting its content. Associations of Christian managers of companies, where there are any, lead a precarious existence. On the other hand, the Rotary Club, the Lions and the Masonic Lodge enjoy a certain prosperity. Is this not symptomatic? Would not the paternalistic philanthropy they practice sometimes serve

[32] J. Terra, "El desafio marxista," in *Mensaje* 115, pp. 146ff.
[33] Cf. the declaration of the central committee of the Brazilian episcopate, quoted in Houtart-Pin, *op. cit.,* p. 213.
[34] R. Vekemans, "Análisis psico-social de la situación pre-revolucionária de América Latina," in *Mensaje* 115, pp. 71-3.

to anesthetize the bad conscience that flees from its real obligations? Far be it from us to put in doubt the sincerity and good faith of others, but even capitalism has its "useful innocents", becoming more numerous with the increasing subtlety of their propaganda in Christian circles.

The ruling class needs a double conversion: a conversion to reality and a conversion to Christ. Only in this way will it discern the signs of the times and discover its mission in a new social order, placing at the service of the people all its cultural patrimony, on the basis of scientific objectivity, technological activity and doctrinal rationale.[35] Many are already close to this conversion. Others, especially of the younger generation, have already passed through this and, in anguish, live a real drama of conscience. But they are also victims of the social order. They are often forced to tolerate dishonest maneuvers in the midst of their enterprises under the threat of economic destruction. But they must not lose sight of their being called to be the leaven in their class, thus preparing the way of the Lord.

4. *The Developed Countries*

The struggle of the Third World toward development is a problem that concerns the whole world. R. Coste points out clearly the stages of the relationship between rich and poor countries: from exploitation to assistance, from assistance to cooperation.[36]

Exploitation still occurs. It manifests itself most of all in the speculation in raw materials on the international commodity markets, in a despoiling form of trade that forces the poor countries to pay high prices abroad for products manufactured from those same raw materials, in the trusts that stifle national industry, etc. Only a trade that obeys an ethic of a world economy, an economy of the species, as F. Perroux says, will be able to defeat the "satellization" of the Third World. The Third World has in fact already

[35] *Ibid.*, p. 73.
[36] R. Coste, *op. cit.*, p. 525.

begun to exert a certain pressure, almost trade-unionist, in this direction.[37]

Technical and financial assistance is given. In *Pacem in terris* John XXIII praises the readiness with which his appeal in *Mater et Magistra* (n. 122) was attended. Government, Churches, private organizations acted, often with impressive detachment. Nevertheless what is given is still little. It should make possible rapid industrial development without restricting overmuch internal consumption which is already uncertain, without rigid restraint of wages, for this creates political tension and the risk of a violent and purely redistributive revolution in a continent already dangerously explosive. What is given is also little in relation to that which could be given. According to the statistics it does not reach 1% of the national income of the rich countries.

These are just crumbs falling from the rich man's table. The rich, meanwhile, slaves to the tyranny of advertising, continue to consume much beyond the limits of what is useful and to defend their tables with the arms race. Should it not be obligatory to turn swords into plowshares, according to the words of the prophet recalled by Paul VI in his address to the United Nations? And is the conquest of space not realized at the cost of the developing countries? Is the present generation not being unduly sacrificed for the future? The little that is given is often misused. Although the birthrate problem exists, a network of birth control clinics is not of great interest to Latin America. There is no lack of room for human life. What are lacking are productive resources. Instead of reducing the number of participants at the banquet of life, rather let bread be given plentifully, according to the happily chosen words of the Pope in that address. The little that is given is often given without a rational plan or does not reach

[37] F. Perroux, "De l'avarice des nations à une économie du genre humain," in *Richesse et Misere, 39e semaine sociale de France* (1952), pp. 195ff.; "La satellisation du tiers monde," in *Economie et Humanisme* 162 (1965), pp. 46ff.; M. Marques Moreira, "Comércio, a juda e desenvolvimento," in *Síntese Política Econômica Social* 6 (1964), pp. 18-37; L.-J. Lebret, "Solidarité internationale et richesses mondiales," in *Economie et Humanisme* 21 (1962), pp. 98ff.

where it should. The little that is given is often given from self-interest despite the grave warning of *Mater et Magistra* against neo-colonialism (n. 171ff.). The price is the imposition of a certain ideology, of certain cultural patterns that are not in harmony with the people being helped. And the due effectiveness of this small amount is put in jeopardy by embezzlers,[38] despite *Mater et Magistra* speaking in terms of rights and duties (n. 158).

The two great world blocs in dispute seek to expand their dominion over the Third World. A revolutionary union movement of Christian inspiration is opposed by both using unfair means. Bishops and priests who preach reform run the risk of being estranged through diplomatic pressure.[39] Any revolutionary surge is immediately stifled under the guise of communist infiltration. It is quite possible that in this way we are playing the dialectic game of those whom we oppose. The stronger the oppression, the greater will be the reaction. Thus, at least, think the great players behind the scenes. The creator of the Alliance for Progress understood in good time and with exceptional clarity of vision that Latin America should be allowed to carry through its revolution. Since his untimely death the chances of a peaceful revolution have noticeably worsened. Hence it is necessary to alert the world's conscience in the face of the uncertainty of the situation. For only through revolution, toward development, can the phase of world cooperation be reached.

Undoubtedly, what is asked of the developed countries is extremely difficult and delicate. An almost superhuman trust is demanded in the constructive forces still latent in the poor countries, still all too vulnerable. An almost heroic patience is demanded in the face of the proverbial political corruption which exists in Latin America and in the face of so many other mistakes, so difficult to remedy. The detachment and generosity demanded, so contrary to man's natural selfishness, will grow only

[38] *Chronique Sociale de France* 72 (1964), pp. 210ff.
[39] The duplicated periodical *SOCI* (*Servicio de Prensa Obrero Campesino Internacional*) published in Chile relates a case of this nature and almost every issue reports cases of union persecution.

from a deep love of man as he is and of all who are of our lineage. Will this be possible without a change of heart? Would not this conversion, this revolution of mankind necessarily lead to a sort of new social revolution in the developed countries themselves?

The wind of change that started in 1775 after having thrice swept over the continents is trying to return to its native lands where, in Toynbee's words, the arch-revolutionary country has become the arch-conservative one.[40] The hour has come for all to understand the signs of the times and to fulfill our historic mission in the building of a new and more human world.

[40] A. Toynbee, *America and the World Revolution*, p. 26.

Yves Congar, O.P./*Strasbourg, France*

Poverty in Christian Life amidst an Affluent Society

To a Christian, the question of the place of poverty in an affluent society is both important and topical. I propose to discuss it by first turning to St. Thomas whose teaching is so evangelical and at the same time so reasonable and human.*

Poverty can be considered as a simple economic fact: the position of a "have-not", the situation of deprivation. Here we can distinguish several degrees which, as is immediately obvious, are not merely a matter of quantity. In the domain of possibilities of human development, quantitative degrees easily become qualitative differences. According to Pius XII, property is the living space of the person. Following the French jurist, J. Hamel,[1] we

---

* Apart from the works and studies quoted in the footnotes, I wish to mention the following books: "Riches et Pauvres dans l'Eglise ancienne" in *Lettres chrétiennes* 6 (ed. by A. Hamman) (Paris: Grasset, 1962); R. Régamey, *La Pauvreté et l'homme d'aujourd'hui* (Paris: Aubier, 1963); E. Roche, *Pauvreté dans l'abondance. Prospérité matérielle et pauvreté évangélique* (Tournai/Paris: Casterman, 1963); Y. Conger, *Pour une Eglise servante et pauvre* (Paris: Ed. du Cerf, 1964); J. Leuwers, L'espérance des milieux pauvres. Textes et témoignages (Paris: Ed. Ouvrières, 1964); G. Mercier and M.-J. Le Guillou, *Mission et Pauvreté* (Paris: Ed. du Centurion, 1964); P. Gauthier, *Consolez mon peuple. Le Concile et "L'Eglise des Pauvres"* (Paris: Ed. du Cerf, 1965); R. Voillaume and Y. Congar (ed.), *Eglise et Pauvreté* (Unam Sanctam [Paris: Ed. du Cerf, 1965]).

[1] J. Hamel, in *Cahiers du Droit* 25 (Dec. 1951), p. 51; I take the quotation from R. Régamey, *La Pauvreté et l'homme d'aujourd'hui* (Paris, 1963), p. 196.

may distinguish four degrees: (1) *misery,* or "the situation of those who do not have enough to provide for those needs that are necessary *for all men*"; (2) the opposite extreme, *richness,* or "the situation of those who, within their environment, possess an abundance of goods, allowing them to indulge in all the superfluities of their liking to a large degree" (this definition, it will be noticed, presents richness as something *relative:* what may be relative ease in one milieu may appear as luxury and richness in another); (3) the *well-to-do,* who have "enough wealth to achieve an average affluence compared with others of their environment, but without appreciable superfluity" (again a relative position); (4) *poverty,* or "the situation of those who cannot manage to achieve the common standard of their environment and who, without lacking the essentials, must deny themselves certain satisfactions that appear normal to those among whom they live".

Taken as such, poverty is not a good, and it is right to seek to escape from it. When it becomes misery, it is even degrading insofar as it prevents a man from realizing his humanity to the fullest degree. Of the four degrees mentioned, misery is the only one that is defined unconditionally and refers to man as such. Clearly, therefore, the struggle to eliminate misery is a duty in the strict sense because of a person's share in mankind, and still more so for the Christian because of the nobility of the human being as presented in the plan of God's creation and redemption.

The situation of a "have-not", then, is not a good in itself, or a virtue, first of all, because virtue is essentially a habit that disposes man toward the good and therefore qualifies as good him who possesses it, and secondly, because virtue is a freely chosen disposition. Therefore, *a priori,* a situation imposed from without and suffered—not chosen—cannot be a virtue. In both the Old and New Testaments, poverty, as an economic condition, appears as indifferent or neutral insofar as communion with God is concerned. Jesus had friends among the rich, but he frequented the poor and the latter were completely at ease with him. The curses he pronounced against the rich were clearly aimed at a certain attachment to riches and the consequences of this attachment with regard to one's behavior toward God and men.

St. Thomas Aquinas found himself forced to examine the questions raised by poverty, not only in the light of his reasonable and well-organized system of virtues, but also in the light of that evangelism that he himself had voluntarily embraced.[2] Although M.-D. Chenu has thrown much light on the evangelism of Aquinas, a systematic study of this evangelism in his *theology* still remains to be done. Such a study would also have to be historical and take note, for instance, of what St. Thomas may have owed to his masters,[3] and especially trace the currents and conflicts of ideas that filled the 13th century. We know that he had to fight on two fronts: against the secular scholars and against a certain absolutization of religious poverty among Franciscan scholars.

For St. Thomas, voluntary poverty was in no sense perfection itself but only a *means* to perfection.[4] According to him the ideal was the common possession of a moderate amount of goods, according to the *specific purpose* of each institution, these goods being acquired and managed in a peaceful way and in due time, so as to reduce preoccupation with them to a minimum.[5] This idea of voluntary poverty as a simple means was attacked by the Franciscans of his day. For them, the actual practice of poverty (*usus pauper*) and the actual lack of possessions were of the essence of the vow of poverty which, without these elements, would tend to become pure fiction.[6] However, Aquinas main-

[2] Young Thomas, indeed, based his vocation on the choice, not of religious life as such (he was destined for Monte Cassino), but of the mendicant life of the first Blackfriars.

[3] The evangelism of the first generations of Dominicans and the evangelism taught currently at the time. Albert the Great characterized the evangelical attitude that allows entry into the fold by truth, voluntary giving, freedom and simplicity, in his commentary on *Ev. Ioan.* X, 1 (ed. Borgnet), p. 396.

[4] Cf. IIa-IIae, q. 184, a.3; 186, a.8; 188, a.7.

[5] Q. 188, a.7. See the still valid conclusions of A. Ott, *Thomas von Aquin und das Mendikantentum* (Freiburg, 1908).

[6] See M. Bierbaum, *Bettelorden und Weltgeistlichkeit an der Universität Paris* (Münster, 1920), p. 367 (Peckham's text); A Dempf, *Sacrum*

tained his position and today the debate seems to be dead and buried.

St. Thomas discussed the question of poverty in different places of the *Summa* according to the various levels of Christian practice. Nothing is more enlightening than to follow this discernment in his procedure, which displays in itself a profound understanding. Thus, we find three levels in Christian practice, not unconnected but organically linked.

1. There is, first of all, the level of the *virtues,* in this case the virtue of prudence[7] that regulates and measures the means according to the aims of charity which is an absolute ("the measure of charity is to love God without measure"), and the virtue of temperance by which we regulate the use of created goods.

2. Next, there is the level of the practice of the evangelical *counsels,* among which is included the practice of voluntary poverty. The *Constitution on the Church* returned here to the perspective of the Gospel—which is also that of St. Thomas' ethics —according to which the counsels are proposed to all the faithful: not imposed on their obedience, like the precepts, but suggested to their supernatural prudence as something to be practiced by each, according to his state and vocation, in view of each man's love of God and neighbor.[8] The practice of the evangelical counsels is therefore not reserved to the religious who make a special and public profession of them, and who pursue this practice in principle in a way of life that is wholly organized, even in its social structure, on the basis of these counsels in order to achieve a more perfect love of God and neighbor.

St. Thomas did not develop his ethics as an imitation of Christ. In general, this ethical system does not look very christological, and people have not failed to reproach him for this. Nevertheless,

---

Imperium (Munich, 1929; Darmstadt, 1934), pp. 338, 350 (Bertrand of Bayonne), p. 340 (Bonaventure and Peckham); D. Douie, *The Nature and the Effect of the Heresy of the Fraticelli* (Manchester, 1932), pp. 83, 96f. (Olivi).

[7] IIa-IIae, q.55, a. 6, 7 and 8.

[8] *Constitution on the Church,* nn. 39f. See H. Feret, "L'Eglise des Pauvres, Interpellation des Riches," in *L'Eglise aux cent visages* 14 (Paris, 1965), pp. 201-28.

he had some very profound reasons for not doing so. The end is union *with God,* conformity *with God,* a veritable divinization. St. Thomas' ethics are wholly dominated by the theological virtues (virtues that have God directly as their object), of which he perceived the theological character more than anyone else.[9] Nevertheless, when it comes to the counsels, particularly the one of voluntary poverty, St. Thomas formally adduces the motive of "following Christ",[10] a specific motive in his mind, and therefore an imitation that has the character of "learning from Christ" and following in his footsteps (*following* rather than only *imitation*).

3. Finally, there is the level of the gifts of the Spirit, that is, of being directly moved by God, according to *his* measure, beyond a regulation derived from *our* view of things and *our* prudence, even the supernatural kind. This is very typical of the Christian ethics of St. Thomas. He gives it full value in his ethics, the end of which is wholly dominated by love and gifts and by the conquest of the freedom of the children of God: "Those that are moved by the Spirit are the children of God." [11] The gifts of the Spirit are dispositions permanently given to us in order that we may follow, with God's grace, the impulse God himself gives us beyond human standards, even virtuous ones, so that we can act fully as children of God according to the views and the degree established by *God.* Now, St. Thomas connects the evangelical practice of voluntary poverty with the gift of fear which, as the beginning of wisdom, has a basic value in religious life and is, according to him, linked with hope.[12] Because of this virtue and this gift, it becomes a matter of achieving perfect submission to

[9] See L. B. Gillon, "L'imitation du Christ et la morale de S. Thomas," in *Angelicum* 36 (1959), pp. 263-86.

[10] For poverty, see IIa-IIae, q.158, a.6 ad 1; q.186, a.3 ad 6, making use of a quotation from S. Prosper's *De ecclesiasticis dogmatibus* (c.38); q.188, a.7: "Perfection does not consist essentially in poverty but in the following of Christ"; IIIa, q.35, a.7 and q.40, a.3.

[11] Rom. 8, 14, a text often quoted by Thomas. See S. Lyonnet and I. de la Potterie, " La vie selon l'Esprit, condition du chrétien," in *Unam Sanctam* 55 (Paris, 1965).

[12] IIa-IIae, q.19, a.12.

God in a perfect and total dependence on him, whether this leads
to the "annihilation of the blown-up and proud mind" [13] or, *via*
a total and unalloyed confidence in God in obedience to the instinct put into us by the Spirit, to an impulse to reject that support
which one might seek and find in temporal goods.[14] The heroic
example of the saints, of the founders, and of so many Christian
men and women at grips with a life of hardship here illustrates
this traditional teaching. At this level, voluntary or accepted
poverty becomes a basic and general value in Christian life, in
a humility that is itself the measure of the depth of all spiritual
life.[15]

The meaning of St. Thomas' teaching is clear: for a Christian
who practices the spiritual life in one way or another, there exists
a level which differs from that of a morality based on reason, even
a reason enlightened by faith, and from the ordinary moral interpretation of things as they are. There is an ethics based on God
such as he has shown himself to us in Jesus Christ, "the way, the
truth and the life" (John 14, 6). At this level it is no longer a
matter of merely regulating our life virtuously in the circumstances in which we are placed in the world, but of critically
examining the sense and truth of our existence before the absoluteness of God and his plan of salvation which culminates in the
wisdom of the cross, wiser than all our planning and all our fore-
sight.

This has always been practiced among the People of God by
souls who, in total surrender to God through defiance of the self,
have set about building the mystical city of which Augustine said:
"Self-love, to the contempt of God, has built the city of evil; the
love of God, to the contempt of the self, has built the city of
God." [16] In ancient Israel this was the law that ruled the existence
of the poor of Yahweh or *anawim*, "that permanent Israel which

[13] *Loc. cit.*, quotation from St. Augustine's *De Sermone Domini in Monte* (P. L. 34, p. 1231).
[14] *Loc cit.*, with reference to St. Ambrose, *Expos. in Luc.* VI, 20 (P. L. 15, p. 1735) and to St. Jerome, *In Matt. 5, 3* (P. L. 26, p. 34).
[15] Cf. IIa-IIae, q.19, a.12; q.18, a.7 ad 3; IIIa. q.40, a.3 ad 3.
[16] *De Civitate Dei* XIV, 28 and XV, 1 (P. L. 41, pp. 456-7).

lives on prayer and expectation . . . striving toward the encounter with God".[17] The *anawim* had their ideal in the Virgin
Mary, and their finest expression of it is in her *Magnificat*. They
are the ones envisaged in the first beatitude: "Blessed are the poor
in spirit, for theirs is the kingdom of heaven" (Matt. 5, 3). That
the *spirit* of poverty cannot exist or last without some move in the
direction of real poverty can be seen from the parallel formula
in Luke, which, according to exegetes such as D. J. Dupont, reproduces the original saying more exactly: "Blessed are you poor.
. . . But woe to you that are rich" (Luke 6, 20. 24).

Today this appeal of the Gospel has been given new strength
not only in exceptional vocations but also in the Christian people
as a whole. We are witnessing a rediscovery of poverty as an
existential value, beyond a simple, morally justified use of earthly
goods.[18] In the middle of a world dominated by the search for the
greatest comfort and material success, there are many Christian
households where the style of life and the education of children
furnish a denial of the primacy of richness and money. Our present age is characterized by a rediscovery of the Christian man,
that is, a man who does not limit himself to professing the faith
and to fulfilling such ethical and liturgical duties as the Church
prescribes, but who tries to live the Gospel *in his very behavior
as man*. A Christian man is a man who shares, who stands open
to others, who serves, who does not decline the appeals of others.
Many households live by those values on the lines and in the
spirit of evangelical poverty. Sometimes these "groups of the
evangelical life" that are on the increase go even further: free
hospitality, involvement in some charitable work, pooling of resources by certain groups and referring their expenses to the
leader, etc. I know of a household with two young children where

[17] A. Gelin, *Les Pauvres de Yahvé* (Paris, 1953), p. 98.
[18] From among the mass of evidence: D. Day, *The Long Loneliness*
(New York, 1960); I. Gobry, *La pauvreté du laïc* (Paris: Ed. du Cerf,
1961); *Les XLmes Journées de la Paroisse Universitaire* (Montpellier,
April 2-5, 1960); special number of the *Cahiers universitaires catholiques:*
"La Pauvreté," (June-July, 1963); *Les Journées des Informations Catholiques Internationales* (Lyons, 1964); cf, *supra,* n. 8.

they follow the rule of not budgeting for more than a month ahead and give away the surplus.

This practical rediscovery of evangelical poverty is linked to the absolute value of love, of *agape,* beyond all moralism, and to the values of service, responsibility and witness. It owes much to the determination not to live for oneself only, but to *be with* the others, particularly with the poorest, to put oneself "at the center of distress, in the heart of misery", to enter into a communal relationship with those that are deprived. It is decisively bound up with the rediscovery of the values of Christian existence or ontology, beyond the moralism or legalism so frequently denounced at Vatican Council II.

The question of poverty cropped up constantly at the Council where it had its prophets and its witnesses. Most of the important conciliar texts display this preoccupation: the Dogmatic *Constitution on the Church,*[19] the Pastoral *Constitution on the Church in the Modern World* and the *Decree on the Ministry and Life of Priests,* among others. Paul VI has repeatedly shown himself worried by this question of poverty as it must be practiced by the Church and Christians. In his encyclical *Ecclesiam Suam* he asked all the bishops for their help and their suggestions.

All this is fine but it does not dispose of all the questions. We must frankly admit that it is the rich—or, in any case, people who are not exactly "needy"—who *talk* about poverty. Sometimes they talk very well indeed, but that does not change anything. They themselves continue to live as before and we have to recognize that it would not be easy for them to do otherwise, for each of them is ensnared in structures and existential conditions that he is practically powerless to change. And yet, our discussion of poverty and the poor ought not to remain confined to ideology, an escape from the real problems, a way of too easily satisfying a bad conscience. In this field nothing could be worse than a false hypocrisy. If we talk of poverty, we have to do so in *realistic* terms if we want to avoid romanticism or hypocrisy. That

---

[19] See J. Dupont's study, "L'Eglise, la Pauvreté et les Pauvres," in *L'Eglise de Vatican II* (the collection edited by G. Barauna; English translation in preparation: London: Burns & Oates).

is why, in the next part of this article, I want to examine in greater detail how the search for the evangelical truth about poverty can and must be expressed: (1) on the level of our personal life, as a quality of our Christian existence; (2) in the way it influences our conduct and our free choices in a world to which we belong and which is at the same time a world of prosperity— even of abundance—and of misery.

1. *Poverty as an Existential Quality in Our Personal Life*

We have seen that many of the faithful have discovered for themselves that the call to poverty is part of the Christian condition. These faithful want to be fully *in* the world, not *of* it, but rather *of* the kingdom of God in their conduct and their style of life. They understand that the life of a Christian demands a reform of judgment and of spirit (see Rom. 12, 2; Eph. 4, 23) and a conversion in depth (*metanoia*). It is a pity that priests do not preach this sufficiently or present it only as a matter of particular practices or a hardly satisfactory moralizing casuistry. One cannot seriously be a Christian without committing himself by this evangelical conversion to the principles by which one lives and in that existential quality which Kierkegaard called a "deepening of existence". It is a matter of dying to the carnal man we are according to the world, and of being born to a certain meaning of life and the world according to God. This does not make us withdraw from the world but commits us to being lost to the world to begin with, in the way the world thinks about itself, and to being returned to the world as God conceives it, the world of the Father. It is then no longer the world where one lives *for one's own enjoyment,* but the world God loved so much that he *gave* his only Son to it and in which he pursues a plan, with Christ as its principle, center and exemplar, for its salvation and fulfillment.[20] To be lost to the world *of the world* and to be born again to the world *of God* means to be committed to a life of spiritual freedom and of service—the condition of which is a certain pov-

[20] On these points see W. Dirks, "Der Welt-verloren und aller Welt-freund," in *Geist und Leben* 23 (1950), pp. 288-98; Y. Congar, *Lay People in the Church* (London: Chapman, 1957); *idem, Les Voies du Dieu vivant* (Paris, 1962), pp. 359-66.

erty. It is to live in the Church as she was born at Easter and
Pentecost, and whose features we can trace in the Acts and the
writings of the apostles. It is to find and put into practice the full
truth of the religious bond that ties us to God and, by the same
token, to our brothers, mankind.

This religious bond is based on faith, hope and charity in such
a way that charity finds its full religious and Christian truth in
faith and hope as its foundation. The example and teaching of
St. Francis of Assisi show this. This example and teaching did
not appear without reason at the time when the modern world
took shape, marked as it was by the passage from a wholly local-
ized land-economy to an economy of commercial exchange—
the circulation of money—thanks to bills of exchange and banks:
in short, to an economy that introduced the realm of capitalism.[21]
The profound meaning of St. Francis' poverty goes well beyond
the poetry of the *Fioretti,* of his marriage to Dame Poverty, and
even beyond the virtues that belong to "the sphere of morality".
His poverty derives from evangelical conversion and from the perfect and absolute realization of a purely vertical dependence on
God.[22] This relationship with God is that of faith and hope pushed
to the point where one wants to depend on God only—and this
in constant actuality—at all moments and in every circumstance
of life. The Gospel illustrates this by the solemn warning of Christ
that "nobody can serve two masters"; one either serves God or
one serves creatures taking the place of God.[23]

[21] On this human situation of St. Francis, born of a wealthy wool
merchant, see L. Hardick, "Franziskus, die Wende der mittelalterlichen
Frömmigkeit," in *Wiss. u. Weisheit* 13 (1950), pp. 129-41; Y. Congar,
Les Voies du Dieu vivant, pp. 247f.; A. Sayous, "L'origine de la lettre
de change," in *Rev. hist. Droit* (1933), pp. 66-112.

[22] Apart from my study referred to in the preceding note, cf. T. Soiron,
"Das Armutsideal des hl. Franziskus und die Lehre Jesu über die Armut,"
in *Franziskanische Studien* 4 (1917), pp. 1-17; C. Drukker, "De evangelische en franciscaanse zin der boetvaardigheid," in *Sint Franciscus
Tijdschrift* 57 (1955), pp. 65-119; the Brothers of the Scholasticate of
Alverne, "Armoede als godsdienstige gesteltenis in de hl. Schrift," *ibid.,*
pp. 130-70, and C. de S. Clasen, "De armoede van S. Franciscus en
het heilig Evangelie," in *Rev. d'Hist. Eccl.* 52 (1957), pp. 366-8.

[23] Matt. 6, 24; Luke 16, 13. The same occurs already in the prophets
Elijah (1 Kgs. 18, 21) and Zephaniah (1, 5) in the overall context of the
true religious relationship. See also Prov. 18, 10-11.

This point becomes much clearer when one looks at the biblical notion of faith, expressed in its original and concrete meaning by the Hebrew use of the word. Hebrew is a concrete language that expresses the most spiritual realities by starting from concrete images. The Hebrew word which expresses the fact of believing derives from the causative form (*hiphil*) of the verb *'aman,* which means "to carry", and therefore, in this form, "to cause to carry". To believe, therefore, means to cause someone else to carry you, and so to lean on someone else, to trust him.[24] The Gospel often talks of Mammon as the opposite of the God on whom we lean in faith. One puts one's trust in Mammon or in God. It is *either* the one *or* the other—it cannot be both. Now, while the etymology of the Aramaic word "Mammon" (which has passed into our language in the way Jesus pronounced it) remains uncertain, there are outstanding biblical scholars who believe that it is linked to the same root *'MN* as the verb *'aman* which expresses the act of faith.[25] If this derivation is correct, Mammon would be precisely that on which man leans and in which he puts his trust in a way that would excuse and even prevent him from leaning on God and putting his trust in God.

In this way poverty becomes the concrete condition of the theological virtues of faith and hope and would itself assume a theological character. It would no longer be concerned merely with the right use of the goods of this world on the horizontal level of life but also with our vertical relationship with God. It becomes part of the condition, or even of the very structure, of our relationship with God. This is undoubtedly the reason why St. Paul assimilates greed with a form of idolatry (Col. 3, 5 and Eph. 5, 5). Faith consists in seeing to it that God is really God for us, the true God, the living God, who wishes to be sovereign in the life of his creatures for their own good. God is really *my* God, the God of my salvation, only if I trust him with the conduct of my life. I cannot let anyone else take the place of "Lord" in his stead.

[24] Our "amen" is an adverb derived from the same root and used as an interjection: "It is worthy of trust" or "This is certain" or *"This is true! I accept it!"*

[25] Thus, E. Hoskyns and N. Davey, *The Riddle of the New Testament,* 3rd ed. (London, 1947), pp. 28f.

In this line of thought we can understand why St. Thomas linked the practice of poverty with the basic dispositions of the fear of God, and of the gift of fear, itself linked with the theological virtue of hope and with humility.[26] From this basic value a whole system of asceticism, a line of conduct, can be derived: the Christian must strive to dominate that sufficiency which, in a carnal way, he tends to find in himself and in all that constitutes for him the spirit of possessiveness or that attachment to possession which would turn him into a slave instead of a free and royal master.[27] And here is the place to insert the whole part played by almsgiving in our conquest of that spiritual freedom in which our *royal* priesthood finds expression. However we must then interpret almsgiving, linked to fasting, as embracing all voluntary impoverishment, the whole conquest of the spirit of possessiveness by the spirit of offering, as Vladimir Solovyev suggested.[28] The conversion of the Christian demands a radical and general criticism of any proprietary attitude.[29]

In the Scriptures, particularly after the incarnation of the Son of God, the truth of our relationship with other men cannot be separated from the truth of our relationship with God. It is even too little to say that the two commandments of love are similar. We must recognize that we cannot fulfill the first if we fail in the second, and even that the second has a kind of practical priority over the practice of the first. Biblically speaking, according to the Gospels particularly, there can be no true recognition of the fatherhood of God without the effective practice of

[26] Cf. *supra,* footnote 12. Christ is born in Bethlehem, not in a proud city, in order to confound the pride of men (IIIa, q. 35, a. 7 ad 1); the pride of Rome, capital of the world, bows down before the humility of Christ and his apostles (*ibid.,* ad 3; q. 40, a. 3 ad 4).

[27] St. Jerome, commenting on Matt. 6, 24ff., writes: "He did not say: 'He who has wealth', but 'He who serves wealth'. For he who serves wealth guards this wealth as a servant, but he who shakes off the yoke of servitude distributes them like a lord" (*P. L.* 26, p. 45).

[28] Cf. V. Solovyev, *The Spiritual Foundations of Life.* Thomas sees poverty in the perspective of vowed poverty, which is, ideally speaking, the gift of *all* (IIa-IIae, q. 186, a. 3 ad 6).

[29] In J. Olier, *Introduction à la vie chrétienne,* ch. XI, section IX, the opposition between the "owner" and the Christian is worked out in successive contrasts in over thirty paragraphs.

brotherhood toward man, just as we cannot go to the limit in the second if we deny the first.

Here again St. Francis of Assisi is our master. I am thinking of that scene where he broke with the carnal world to give himself up to life according to the Gospel. He had begun to commit himself to this life but still retained the disposal of family wealth which he dissipated with chivalrous carelessness and prodigality. His shocked father was concerned about this; he asked the bishop to summon Francis and to make sure that he would return the rest of his money. In front of the bishop, Francis threw off his clothes and put them at his father's feet with the solemn declaration: "Let everyone listen and understand. Up till now I have called Pietro de Bernardone my father. But as I have decided to serve only God from now on, I return to Pietro de Bernardone the money he was worried about and all the clothes I received from him. Henceforth, I shall no longer be able to say, 'My father Pietro de Bernardone,' but 'Our Father, who art in heaven.' " [30] There we have God recognized as the Father whom one expects to provide all things because he takes care of his creatures.[31] Here we also have the relation of brotherhood which St. Francis saw as deriving from God's fatherhood, and we understand now that he extended it literally, and not just poetically, to animals and plants. One day a brother asked St. Francis permission to have a psalter. The saint replied: "When you have your psalter, you will want a breviary. And when you have a breviary, you will sit down on a chair like a fat prelate and you will say to your brother: 'Bring me my breviary.' " [32]

The position of St. Francis was an extreme one, deriving from that unparaphrased, literal and zealous reading of the Gospel which, ultimately, he did not impose on others. Nevertheless, his attitude undeniably reflects the light of the Gospel. It is a

[30] J. Joergensen, *Saint Francois d'Assise. Sa vie et son oeuvre*, 3rd ed. (Paris, 1909), p. 68.

[31] Matt. 6, 25-34; these texts of the Sermon on the Mount are quoted in the *Regula non bullata*, n. 14 (ed. Boehmer, *Analekten z. Gesch. des Franziskus von Assisi*, Tübingen/Leipzig, 1904, pp. 13f.).

[32] *Legenda antiqua*, nn. 69-79 (ed. F. Delorme, 1926), pp. 40-2; *Speculum perfectionis* 4 (ed. P. Sabatier), p. 11.

fact that possession is the root of the lust for power. Attachment to money corrupts the human heart and destroys there the very possibility of a sense of brotherhood. Anyone of us has but to look around and search his memory or experience: family quarrels, social injustice, lack of worry about the misery and humiliating conditions of others, callousness—all these derive, like a monstrous progeny, from attachment to money. It is the idolatry of the most hollow and ephemeral idol and, instead of faith and hope in our Father, it engenders fratricide.

There is no doubt that the practice of poverty cannot be separated from a Christian life which lives on the level of the ontology of grace and its requirements, beyond a simple moralism.

2. *Our Choice and Conduct in a World of Affluence and Misery*

Our world is indeed one of both affluence and misery. In recent years efforts have been made to rouse the conscience of peoples and the well-to-do classes that live (at least partially) in what has been called the affluent society[33] to a realization of the profound poverty, and even the genuine misery, of a section —we may even say the majority—af mankind.[34] Let us remind ourselves of a few figures. About 150 million families live in subhuman conditions which make it impossible for man to develop himself, while 30 million families live in prosperous countries. Two-thirds of the world's population cannot get the daily 2,500 calories which they need, and 30 million people die each year of starvation, a figure not reached by any war, no matter how atrocious. In India children die at the rate of 185 per thousand; life expectancy there is only 32 years, and 83.4 percent of the population is illiterate. The nineteen richest nations —having the largest proportion of baptized Christians and representing only 16 percent of the world's population—control

[33] J. K. Galbraith, *The Affluent Society.*

[34] See Cardinal Suenens, Cardinal Heenan, Msgr. Ligutti and P. de Lestaples, *Christian Responsibility and World Poverty* (ed. by A. McCormack) (London, 1963); the studies of H. Bartoli (pp. 52-73) and F. Perroux (pp. 86-8) on poverty in rich countries in *La Pauvreté* (mentioned in note 18), and the study by G. Blardone in *L'Eglise des pauvres* (*supra,* note 8).

75 percent of the world's revenue. The nations of the world as a whole each year spend 120 billion American dollars on armament, which is half the gross capital of the world.

This is clearly absurd and unacceptable. If a nation's honor is measured by the way it treats its poor, one has to admit that there is no honor in our society, even in our so-called "Christian" societies. They simply are not Christian, or even humanist, as F. Perroux states, "because natural humanism demands that man not destroy man by sacrificing him to money" (on p. 81 of the article quoted in footnote 34). Christianity has failed to prevent societies that glory in their spiritual heritage from yielding to the power of money and from basing their economy not on the widest service of the greatest number of men, but on the highest profit of a few. We deserve only too well the reproach made by G. Bernanos: "God did not choose the same men to preserve his Word and to fulfill it." [35] The Word which we shall have preserved will condemn us if we do not at the same time fulfill it: "I condemn you out of your own mouth, wicked servant," or, as P. Evdokimov put it: "It is the Church that has the message of deliverance, but it is others that do the delivering." [36]

The scandal has existed for a long time, but today it is out in the open, exposed to the conscience of all since, with modern means of communication, everyone has become present to everyone else. We know the figures of hunger and the statistics of misery; we have seen the photos of children with their swollen bellies, their hollow eyes and their prominent knees between thighbones as thin as the shinbones. On the other hand, the hungry and the wretched have seen the affluence of our installations, our way of life, our luxuries, our tanks and our guns. The Christian tradition had not yet known such a situation which demands a response from the People of God. Neither Thomas Aquinas nor Antoninus of Florence, who tried to bring some morality to the beginnings of capitalism in the 15th century, has

[35] *Lettre aux Anglais,* p. 245.
[36] *La femme et le salut du monde* (Paris, 1958), p. 18.

known anything like it. It is therefore not sufficient to continue repeating the conclusions they reached.

Nor is it good enough that we have rediscovered—and perhaps even practice—poverty as a spiritual value. "One cannot [even] understand the secret" of this poverty "except by relating it to the real poverty, as we relate it to humility and faith".[37] If we failed to do this, poverty as a religious attitude would have no value whatever as a sign and no relation with the world in which we live. Neither faith nor charity allows us to wash our hands of communion with this world, and our finest spiritual attitudes would run the danger of becoming mere neo-pharisaism and scandal.

It is true—and it cannot be repeated too often—that it is not enough to rediscover or even to practice poverty in spirit in our relationship with God. It must be said just as forcibly that this rediscovery and this practice cannot be divorced from our conduct with regard to human misery; they are rather a necessary part of an effective commitment to the struggle against this misery. It is not merely a matter of apostolic usefulness, of making our witness and our word effective. This aspect is of course most important. But only a certain practice of poverty will make the poor listen to us. As Paul Ricoeur said: "It is impossible to be with the poor without being against poverty." Only a Church converted to the poor, and therefore to poverty, can again become truly the Church of the poor. It has been rightly said that, in a Church which has really again become the Church of the poor, the rich will find and take their place, but the poor will never find and take their place in a Church of the rich.

The usefulness, the apostolic necessity, is obvious but, as in this whole article, there is something much more ontological. I have already tried to show something of it: the very truth of our relation toward God obliges us to something with regard to our brothers. "He who says that he loves God and does not love his brothers is a liar" (1 John 4, 20). It is precisely *because*

[37] H. Bartoli, in the study mentioned in n. 34, p. 48.

Christ submitted himself as Son to God his Father that he came down to our poverty and embraced it so that he could deliver us from it. This is the meaning of the incomparably profound hymn of the Epistle to the Philippians (2, 5-11). Thus, spiritual poverty, in the sense I have explained it, commits us to God's plan, and God wishes that man should live and that we should be his collaborators in his providence. It is one of the ways in which redemption encompasses creation, and therefore the reason why it is impossible for the Christian to belong truly to God without belonging effectively to the world. Our spiritual poverty demands that we be active with regard to material poverty and human misery.

On the other hand, effective action in the fight against misery presupposes that one has overcome the instinct of possessiveness and its proprietary attitudes. That is obvious. One can only help the poor effectively to rise above their subhuman condition by attacking the structures of their impoverishment from which the rich profit, even if they do not realize it or do not desire it. One can only serve them when one has judged and eliminated that natural feeling of superiority which causes us to use them for our affluence and to profit, in fact, by their inferiority and their poverty. It is impossible to hoist two-thirds of mankind out of their state of undernourishment if one refuses to touch in any way the living standards of the rich, or the economic system which, by itself, works for the increasing enrichment of the rich and the increasing impoverishment of the poor. World economy cannot possibly find and fulfill its true purpose, and world production cannot possibly stop enriching the rich and dehumanizing the poor, if the rich do not accept a certain impoverishment and other economic and social structures than those that are, in fact, tending toward their own enrichment with the fatal consequence that the poor are maintained in their poverty and even driven further into it.

The example of the Communist countries has shown that the situation can be reversed to the advantage of the poor and the detriment of the rich by an economic and social revolution which is alien and even hostile to any religion because it is taken for granted that religion can only support structures by which the big ones oppress the little ones. It is an established fact that communism has set up, on the level of whole populations, a social system almost wholly free from the motives of personal profit and the pursuit of money.[38] We think that this result has been achieved by force, at least insofar as hostile elements are concerned, and that it is still bound up today with grave denials of personal liberty and dignity as well as with very serious limitations. This we reject. But this fact, however important, in no way excuses us from the duty to fight human misery effectively in the name of God; on the contrary, it makes this duty more urgent. It is in the name of the living God, in the name of the truth of our relationship with him, that we can do no less, though with means very different from those of communism and its compulsion, to overcome misery and the profit motive which engenders it. This is the challenge that the present age addresses to Christians and, in spite of their unworthiness, through them to God.

We must clearly understand to what this commits Christians as the People of God. It seems that one might envisage the Christian response in three stages, progressively widening and becoming more demanding.

1. The Christian must build up an attitude and an action that might be called revolutionary, in the sense to be explained further on. He is not first of all a revolutionary: as Dostoievski expressed it so well, the revolutionary is interested in what is distant, the Christian in what is near. The revolutionary sacrifices persons to the building up of his system and is not stopped by the sight of tears and blood as long as, through them and beyond them, another generation may reach a situation where

---

[38] The scientific and Christian economist, F. Perroux, shows this when he writes: "If you visited Moscow you would not have the impression of poverty; you would notice a certain austerity, perhaps dangerous, and certainly controlled by the police, but at least *outwardly* reminding one of *a Christian society that would take the basic articles of its faith and morals seriously*" (referred to in n. 34, p. 83).

such tears and blood will no longer flow. Charity not only keeps an eye on the distant future but is concerned with the here and now. It wants first of all to relieve the most urgent and the most immediate misery. It is not systematic but concrete. That is why almsgiving (which can take other forms than giving a coin to a beggar) keeps a value of which no demand for efficiency can deprive it, in the Christian response to the questions raised by the existence of the poor. However, we must recognize, as Ozanam and Armand de Melun did in the last century, that this is but the beginning of a response, and the truth of both our charity and the issues raised by poverty demands that we aim, beyond the immediate, at the root causes of world poverty. If any effective response demanded of us by the poverty of others implies, on our part, the acceptance of a certain impoverishment (which presupposes that we have begun to practice spiritual poverty), this does not hold only on the level of individual and occasional almsgiving but also on that of wider, better planned and more technical operations.

2. The present situation obviously demands such operations, and therefore the Christian must, without neglecting immediate and particular cases of distress, translate today the law of almsgiving into terms that correspond to the immensity and urgency of poverty, to the unification of nations and conditions all over the world, to the knowledge we have of the causes of impoverishment, to the general historical movement of the nations, to their determination to improve their underdevelopment, and, lastly, to the universal character of the human and spiritual needs that are at stake. Almsgiving—the word is so loaded with condescension and a presupposed immobility of society that I prefer to say: the service which Christians must render to the poor of the world today—lies in helping them effectively to eliminate their poverty, their underdevelopment and, for many, their subhuman conditions, by bringing to them such disinterested aid as will *provide them with the means to vanquish this poverty.* This implies education, instruction, planning, the training of technicians and of teams. Given equal value in technical terms, Christians can do this better than others. They can bring to it a spirit of brotherly

and disinterested service, of a friendship that stands open to all men without an eye on any commercial or imperialist advantage. Insofar as they themselves are those true Christian *men* I mentioned above, they will be conscientious, loyal and dedicated to truth and justice at all costs; without pretending to have the monopoly of these qualities, Christians can bring a humanist and total vision to this undertaking of development and humanization. Planning technicians who would only be technicians might fail to see their work in its totality; by looking at only one or other particularly interesting sector, they might forget the human being or even whole other sectors. Christianity, at least in its present self-awareness, would normally imply such a humanist vision.

3. Commitment to technically effective brotherly aid in overcoming poverty already implies the necessity to fight the mechanisms and structures that tend to consolidate and even worsen the impoverishment of the poor and to keep them in a situation of subjection and exploitation where they have hardly the wherewithal to keep themselves alive in order to provide the capitalist machine, which exploits them, with indispensable labor. And so, they have neither the means nor the possibility, nor even the notion to raise themselves to a life of freedom and conditions that are worthy of a human being. This knowledge of the mechanisms by which the rich exploit the poor, this denunciation of everything that encourages misery and prevents millions of human beings from receiving the instruction, dignity, welfare and freedom to which a man is entitled, and, lastly, the fight against the worship of money which is idolatry—all this is also a general duty for Christians who belong to a world of security and affluence and so are involved in the abuses of the system that gives them these advantages and in the misery of such a vast number of their brothers.

Our age is marked at the same time by both an awareness of the extent of misery in a unified world and by a rediscovery of poverty as a Christian existential value. The two facts are bound to meet, the first somehow leading to the second, which nevertheless has its own sources. The effective commitment to the fight against the misery and subhuman condition of the poor on a world scale demands of Christians that they revise their outlook on things, that they criticize clearly and courageously many ideas to which they were accustomed, and that they accept beforehand a revision (leading to their own impoverishment) of the privileged situation they enjoy. Once again, the necessary transformation can be brought about violently by a Communist kind of revolution, involving a total rupture with all that this implies in the way of destruction. Can it be brought about progressively? An economist has observed: "Never in the history of the West has it been seen that a nation or class, in whatever social system, agreed to lower its living standards for the sake of relieving contemporary misery." [39] It is true that the popes, the theologians, Christian economists and social study weeks have said everything—and said it well—that could and should be said about richness: it is there for the service of man. The Pastoral *Constitution on the Church in the Modern World* forcibly repeats these statements and those of the whole Christian tradition about the human and fraternal purpose of labor and of all possessions (Part II, ch. 3). How could such teaching be effectively translated into facts? It would need technical interventions, a new approach on the level of economic study and a less timid criticism of the situation, not to mention the "establishment", imagination and some daring, without those who undertake such things having to fear that they will be disapproved of, suspected, arrested or condemned, or even simply kept apart from the conformist mass of people who claim the monopoly of approval and confidence. We have now reached the point where Christians are really challenged. They can only face this challenge if at long last they put their own principles into real practice.

How will they redeem the weakness by which they allowed money to reign supreme in Christian countries? As F. Perroux has said, we must devalue wealth and deprive money of all honor (cf. footnote 34). Many Christian families already live and

[39] H. Bartoli, *op. cit.* (n. 34), p. 85.

bring up their children by a standard of values where money does not come first. In this way they make themselves free from the insistence of a mere profit economy which is not connected with needs and which keeps itself going by madly stimulating desires through an obsessive and compelling publicity.[40] Priests have cut the link that existed between certain acts of their ministry and the giving of money. We cannot do without money and the Gospel does not dispense us from that realism which tells us the cost of a ton of cement or a year of study for a seminarian or a missionary. However, there is a brotherly, communal, human and Christian way of conceiving and organizing the economic life of the Church in a manner which, while using money as a means, does not proceed as if money comes first.

The Dogmatic *Constitution on the Church*[41] twice calls the People of God a "messianic people". What can that mean if not a people that brings hope for mankind? In fact, it says that this People of God is a seed of unity and peace, a sign and an instrument of salvation for all mankind. Should this remain mere verbiage or have validity only on the purely spiritual level? But the spiritual element and the eschatology of biblical revelation imply certain effects or anticipations on this earth. The meaning of history is what men make of it, and this is to strive after the kingdom which God will give. People will only believe us if our practical works bear witness to our faith and our charity. The spiritual or evangelical poverty of which God speaks in our hearts today is by itself a religious value. It is meant to allow and sustain an effective service to the poor all over the world, a world in which one-third of the people live in ease and affluence side by side with the two-thirds that live in a poverty and a condition unworthy of man.

[40] On this, see V. Packard, *The Wastemakers*.
[41] Ch. 2, n. 9. Cf. in the collection edited by G. Barauna (note 19) the study by O. Semmelroth, and my two papers given at the 18th *Semaine missiologique espagnole* at Burgos in August, 1965.

Alois Müller/*Fribourg, Switzerland*

Authority and Obedience in the Church

The Christian who has to shape his life and fulfill his tasks on a basis of personal responsibility finds himself confronted in the Church by a twofold authority, an authority of truth and an authority of command. His progress from a freedom demanded by his human nature and his consequent personal responsibility toward action with regard to the world and to his fellowman lead him through the test of ecclesiastical authority. It therefore has its place in the overall picture of Christian freedom and responsibility.

Elements Involved in the Problem

"Ecclesiastical authority" is based on the dogmatic teaching about the function of government, founded by Christ. In order to see it in its true perspective it must, therefore, be defined, explained and marked off in the light of dogma. Once we recognize its true nature in this way, we can study the relation between authority and obedience in the light of a general morality of obedience, where we have to examine whether ecclesiastical obedience and command follow laws of their own. When we have arrived in this way at a "general morality of ecclesiastical command and obedience", it must be put in the context of some concrete contemporary problems, because only then can its relevance become clear for the present-day Christian.[1]

[1] What follows is based on my study, *Das Problem von Befehl und Gehorsam im Leben der Kirche* (Einsiedeln, 1964), which contains and discusses the relevant bibliography (quoted as *Problem . . .*)

71

I

OFFICIAL AUTHORITY AND OBEDIENCE IN THE CHURCH

There are in a certain sense vertical and horizontal levels in the official authority of the Church. Horizontally, an official utterance may contain the authority of truth and/or the authority of command; vertically, official actions may fall within the sphere of either fallibility or infallibility. The qualification "fallible" or "infallible" properly applies to the utterances of the "truth" or teaching authority; in the field of command it finds only a derived application insofar as the pronouncement of a practical (moral) teaching contains a command.

(A) Within the whole field of the teaching authority, the concept of obedience should not really be used at all, but only the concept of *consent*. Obedience is classically defined as a readiness of the will to fulfill a command. It lies in an active attitude or deed of man, based on his will. But in the matter of consent to a truth (teaching), the procedure does not essentially lie in an act of the will but in that of a receptive mind, in an acknowledgement which corresponds to the reality of the teaching. The *consent* of the will to this acknowledgement is inevitable when this acknowledgement is compelling, based on an insight (evidence); it is not inevitable, and therefore free, when the acknowledgement does not lead to an insight but to a probability. No consent is possible when there is a *contradiction* between insight and teaching.

1. The intelligibility or probability of a teaching can spring from two sources: either the immediate and inherent understanding which can verify a statement, or the indirect conclusion based on the competence and trustworthiness of whoever proposes the teaching. In this second case an inherent immediate judgment is again possible, not about the matter itself, but about the actual credibility of the "witness" to the teaching.

2. By its nature the ecclesiastical teaching authority is concerned with questions for which there is no immediate evidence: the teaching of faith which rests upon divine revelation. Its

nature is to proclaim the teaching of the faith under definite conditions with absolute competence. These are the conditions of the infallible proclamation of the teaching. In this case the consent to the teaching, which presupposes the Christian faith, becomes a theoretical necessity for understanding. But since this is not a matter of direct evidence, the consent rests upon an act of the will, and so one can speak of a moral obligation to consent to the faith, but this cannot be identified with an act of obedience.

3. Whenever, then, the ecclesiastical teaching authority does not speak with absolute competence, whether in the case of utterances that do not concern the matter of revelation or when the conditions for infallibility are not fulfilled (statements on faith and morals, the highest doctrinal authority, binding on the whole Church), consent is not in principle a theoretical necessity for understanding, although this may occur in isolated cases. Consent then depends on available ways of understanding: a moral (human) certainty, a greater or lesser degree of probability. But there is also room for legitimate doubt or even evidence to the contrary, because what is not infallible might well be false.

There is, however, a moral duty to act according to one's knowledge. And so, the Christian knows different degrees of moral obligation to base his action on (not infallible) doctrinal utterances of ecclesiastical authority, according to the degree of reliability or probability they possess. However, such a duty, again, belongs to the morality concerned with knowing the truth and cannot be identified with "obedience".

If the fact of an ecclesiastical utterance in general has a certain weight in the balance of probabilities, particularly if the Christian is not theologically competent, nevertheless one cannot turn it into a mechanical argument in cases where other valid arguments enter the picture.

Therefore, the case of contradictory probability or even evidence (however rarely this may occur), there is, consequently, also the duty *not* to base one's action on an ecclesiastical statement.

(B) The attitude toward the *command authority in the Church* presupposes everything that has been said about the doctrinal authority, but implies still other factors. Since I shall deal with the moral issues in themselves in the next section, I confine myself here to the general outline.

In sound theology one cannot attribute infallibility to the command authority, the "pastoral authority", of the Church. One can therefore only speak of infallibility in matters that concern the acknowledgement of unchangeable truths in doctrinal matters, and not in matters of command which are concerned with changeable and concrete situations. On the other hand, even a command cannot break through doctrinal infallibility. This could only happen when a pastoral command with the same authority (binding force) as an infallible doctrine would contradict this doctrine. Even to build up such a case would already be difficult.[2] Presupposing all this, we can envisage the following three situations:

1. An ecclesiastical command may be the immediate outcome of an infallible teaching. In this case it is basically a matter of obedience to a divine command.

2. An ecclesiastical command can be of a purely disciplinary kind, given for the sake of ordering the Church's life. Then we have a problem of obedience in the fullest sense of the word.

3. A command can be the consequence and application of a non-infallible teaching. In that case, what has been said about *consent* remains valid. However, specific questions of moral *obedience* may occur insofar as the knowledge situation in given circumstances leaves the moral freedom to base one's action on this knowledge or not.[3]

[2] Cf. *Problem* . . . , pp. 113-6.
[3] Details about cases discussing the question of intellectual adherence and the right of the member without official function to his own judgment may be found, *ibid.,* pp. 98-124.

II

THE MORAL THEOLOGY OF ECCLESIASTICAL OBEDIENCE

There exists a command authority in the Church, and the question concerns what laws govern the corresponding "ecclesiastical obedience". However, this question cannot be answered without a closer look at the *morality of obedience in general*.

(A) According to the classical definition of obedience, already mentioned, obedience is the readiness to fulfill the commands of a superior (cf. St. Thomas, *Summa Theologica* IIa-IIae, q.104, a.2). But we cannot accept without question this strictly formal definition, since we run the risk of not doing justice to the various angles of this question. We have to delve into the depth of this definition in order to expand this point of view.

1. As a spiritual and free person man faces God in the situation in which he must work out his God-given purpose in life, his "eternal law", on the basis of his own understanding and in freedom of decision. This "obedience to God" is the fundamental task of human existence, penetrating all his activity. Man must fulfill something of the "eternal law"; he must act according to his being.

It is an aspect of human nature that man must often act in human interchange, in the community, and for reasons of order in this activity, this happens in a relationship between superior and subordinate. And so, the action of one is determined by the command of another. This is a relationship of command and obedience. It is clear that the meaning of this lies in the fact that in some way some good of the eternal law is brought about, and that it is not an end in itself. But the command-obedience relationship may be a necessary means toward the sound working out of the eternal law. This means that the basic rules which govern the morality of command and obedience must be derived from the fulfillment of the eternal law, and that secondary rules are concerned with the sound functioning of this relationship. Therefore, when we no longer look at the whole question in a too narrow and formal light, it is obvious that we should not speak exclusively of a "morality of obedience" but rather of a "morality of the relationship between command and obedience", and this embraces the duties of both the one that commands and the one who obeys.

2. The one who gives an order has, first of all, the obligation to see to it that the deed which arises from this coordination of command and obedience corresponds to the eternal law. He can give the order because some objective good can be achieved only by the giving of an order and its execution by someone else. His main intention in the order must therefore be the achievement of such a good. Such an intention would be contradicted by arbitrariness, or giving orders for purely subjective reasons, or the satisfaction of one's own wishes regardless of the objective good. Every superior is exposed to the temptation of the "cardinal vice" of his position: to believe that authority gives him the power and the right to impose binding injunctions on his subordinates for the satisfaction of all his own wishes, pet ideas, etc. On the contrary, in order not to fail in the objective good of the eternal law, he needs to approach the whole situation of the problem with great circumspection, particularly with orders that have far-reaching consequences, and he should be just as skeptical about his own emotional view of things as his subordinate.

The objective good is not always and in all things best achieved by giving definite orders. To allow a situation to develop freely often leads to better prospects so that the best comes out and is achieved. Thus, one of the virtues of a superior should be a right kind of asceticism toward giving orders which leads him to give an order only where it imposes itself as the best method to achieve the objective purpose, and to leave it to free development and the decision of the subordinate when this offers better prospects.

This requirement already belongs partly to the other segment of his task: the creation of a good relationship between authority and obedience. As will be seen later, the subordinate, too, must bear responsibility for his obedience. The superior must make this easier for him by ensuring two essential conditions: trust in the competence, honesty and integrity of his order and the best possible explanation of his order. In many cases this demands that the problem be discussed with the subordinate and the working out together of what then becomes the ordered action.

Since the meaning of the relation between command and obedience lies in the realization of an objective good, it becomes at once an *indebitum* (a non-duty) when this principal aim is compromised by a bad order. Even then it might still remain necessary, operative and compulsory insofar as the suspension of the order might bring about even worse consequences. Nevertheless, the cause of the evil of disobedience lies with the superior to the degree in which the order was objectively unsuitable.

3. *The one who obeys* is bound to the objective good of the eternal law as much as the superior. It is precisely that which is the basis of his duty to obey. The fact that he himself has not decided upon the action but has taken it over as an order does not relieve him of responsibility for his action. The only exception would be the case of someone who was (in whatever sense) "under age". The adult obeys, but in obeying he acts and is responsible for this action.

This responsibility concerns, first of all, the objective contents of the order. The subordinate must always keep his judgment alert as to whether he cooperates toward an objective good. Ignatius' idea about mental obedience, according to which the subordinate should yield to the judgment of his superior unless he is quite clear about the opposite,[4] is not really valid, at least as a general principle of moral obedience. Accessibility to the argument of the superior is a matter of trusting the competence of the superior when emotional obstacles have been truly set aside.

Once the subordinate recognizes that an order impairs the objective good (which is not the same as or runs counter to his

[4] Cf. *ibid.*, pp. 139-53.

own wishes), then his co-responsibility demands that he remonstrate with the superior within the scope of his opportunities and that he try to obtain a better order. This attitude does not arise from a lack of obedience, but rather from a strong determination to obey, which implies the recognition of his share in responsibility.

The readiness to obey, therefore, does not simply cease when the subordinate judges that he cannot agree with what has been commanded. The reason for this is that the relation between order and obedience, particularly in an institutional framework, is so important and necessary to human society that it cannot, for its own sake, be allowed to break down, even when in an individual case it fails to achieve the objective good. This high appreciation of its own inherent value has led to the rule that the subordinate must remain bound to obedience as long as it is not established that the order is a "sin". This is a bad rule because it simplifies unduly the many-sided question of how to weigh up the various goods at issue. Even when the order is not actually a "sin", it can constitute a considerable evil and, in certain circumstances, a worse evil than an individual breakdown in the relation between command and obedience. Therefore, the rule should rather be that, after fruitless attempts to obtain a better order, the subordinate remains obliged to obedience for the sake of the order unless the disturbance of the relationship between command and obedience should lead to something better or is a lesser evil than the execution of a bad order.[5] But just as the superior must beware of arbitrariness in his commands, so the subordinate must beware of arbitrariness in his obedience, considering only his own pet notions in judging the thing to be done and not taking into account the overall view of the objective good. Moreover, just as the superior must ease the mutual relationship through trustworthiness, so must the subordinate do so through willingness to trust and a basically positive attitude. In fact, it is not often a matter of a choice between a good order and a bad one. It is much more often the

[5] For more detailed explanations, see *ibid.*, pp. 168-71.

case of two justifiable points of view with regard to the same problem. An intelligent subordinate should not expect of the superior that he will always give the best possible orders; on the other hand, he should be ready to obey in the whole field of "possible" orders even if he would himself have given another order.

(B) After these general principles of moral theology the question arises as to whether the same principles which have been explained are also valid and a basis for judgment in the case of command and obedience in the Church, or whether ecclesiastical obedience is something different from "natural" obedience.

1. In general, one can say that "ecclesiastical obedience" is in fact either obedience to God—namely, when the Church simply proclaims God's command—or obedience to fellowmen —in which case the above-mentioned principles are valid.[6] The fact that the ecclesiastical official is "God's representative" does not affect the situation in the least because, according to Romans 13, 1, every legitimate authority is the representative of God.

2. The relation between order and obedience in the Church has, however, a "supernatural qualification"; it rests on grace, is a relation within the Church's supernatural community of love, and is a special aspect of the relation of the Church to Christ. Every superior in the Church represents objectively the Lord Christ in the Church, and for every subordinate the act of obedience is a *sign* of his obedience to Christ. The deepest mystery, therefore, of the relation between order and obedience in the Church is the *encounter with Christ*. But the symbolic, quasi-sacramental nature of this mystery should not be wrongly interpreted. It is erroneous to hold that every command given in the Church, as well as its content, is simply a command of God. It *should* be given "in Christ's name", but whether it is so in content and purpose depends as much on the superior as it depends on the subordinate to make his obedience a pledge of his obedience to Christ. Both are something to achieve, but

[6] Cf. *ibid.*, pp. 172-6.

neither is a fact. The human command and obedience in the Church are, as it were, the matter, which must become the sign and receptacle of a higher reality, but they do not presuppose this reality in themselves.

3. The concept of ecclesiastical obedience demands still further analysis. Within the Church there have been two currents of obedience in existence for a long time. The first existed from the beginning, namely, subordination to the Church's authority. The second is the obedience of the monk.[7] The monk turns his whole existence into a sign of the Christian's complete surrender to God. As a sign of the fact that God is the highest good, he abandons all earthly goods in poverty. As a sign that God is the supreme "Thou" of love, he abandons the loving communion of marriage. He does both these things in complete surrender of his own will to God. For this surrender he also has a sign: through his vow the monk renounces the further determination of his life by binding himself to a "rule", and within this rule to a superior. In this monastic obedience he turns all his actions into signs of his obedience to Christ.

This monastic or, in the Romance languages, "religious" obedience (religious life = life in a religious order) is essentially the same as the ecclesiastical obedience described above, but the form it takes is different: not everyone who is subject to general ecclesiastical or "hierarchical" obedience makes it the specific form of his life as does the monk who is the Christian practicing the counsels in a state of life approved by the Church. For this reason hierarchical obedience cannot be simply conceived in terms of religious obedience. The Christian in the world undoubtedly has his pastor in the ecclesiastical community in the person of his ecclesiastical superior, but this superior is not his "religious" superior. The ordinary Christian must also surrender to God's will in all things, but he does not do this permanently under the sign of religious obedience to a fellowman.

4. After these explanations we can see how the morality of

[7] Cf. ibid., pp. 178-87.

command and obedience applies to general ecclesiastical relations. Insofar as ecclesiastical commands are not concerned
with the (infallible) proclamation of God's commands or eventual (not infallible) expansion thereof—in which cases, what I
have said in the first section applies—these commands concern
the life of the Church as a religious (in the broad sense) community. They regulate matters of worship, the proclamation of
teaching, the relations within the Church, and the relations of
the Church and of individual Christians with other institutions.
In the case of the clergy and of religious orders these commands
may affect the whole pattern of life; in the case of the laity they
only affect what is specifically ecclesiastical-religious, insofar as
faith, morals and worship are concerned.

In this field all that has been said about the general morality
of command and obedience is valid, but it is valid in a way
which is supernaturally deeper or on a higher level. The superior
must consider himself bound more seriously to the objective
aim and be more aware of the danger of arbitrariness, since
this aim is always the kingdom of God and his command must
remain valid before Christ whom he is supposed to represent.
He will stimulate the sound functioning of the relation between
command and obedience better by competence, trustworthiness
and explanation of his requests, as he realizes that this relationship must always be a "sacrament" of encounter with Christ in
love, and that his subordinates do not only share as members
of Christ's body in his responsibility but also in a certain
supernatural insight.

This sharing in responsibility and supernatural competence
demands of the subordinates that they take their contribution to
the best command seriously. When they have to contend for
this, and when it is a borderline case, they should be allowed
to refuse obedience when it is clear that, even within the Church,
less harm would be done by this refusal than by obeying an
irresponsible command. When a subordinate says "no" to a
bad command, he obeys Christ, and even represents Christ.

Above all, the subordinate should try to enhance the relation between command and obedience as such by looking on it as a task of love in the body of Christ. This means that he must learn to meet his pastor with love. In an authoritarian régime subordinates fall into a habit of reluctant submission, but indifference, antipathy and contempt separate them completely from their superiors on the human level. Such an attitude is indefensible in the Church, however fallible the superior may be. A love that binds, supports and forgives is not only always a duty in the Church but the highest privilege. It is here that the mystery of the cross shows itself. It is no doubt false to rush into an appeal to the cross when obedience is demanded and so to give the superior *carte blanche* to give any orders he likes, however bad. Nor does the mystery of the cross dispense with the right and duty to insist to the utmost on a good order or to refuse obedience if necessary. Nevertheless, it remains just as much true that the subordinate's love may never cease, and that it must be capable of turning the situation of the worst possible command into grace for the Church in the strength of the cross.

III

CONTEMPORARY PROBLEMS ABOUT COMMAND AND OBEDIENCE IN THE CHURCH

This section will serve to round off the abstract discussion. When we speak of this kind of problem on the "contemporary" level, it is difficult to see where to draw the line. Too much has already been changed since the beginning of the Council to refer to the immediate past before the Council as "contemporary" without qualification. On the other hand, very recent problems created by the awakening of the Church cannot be described simply as "contemporary" either. The present condition of the Church is much better described as one of transition from a past way of life to a future one, and we must therefore try to see the problems of command and obedience in the light of this transition.

(A) The period between World War II and Vatican Council II undoubtedly created problems about authority in the Church. This is already clear from the many references to this question by the pope of that period, Pius XII, and a still growing literature on the subject.[8] The crux of the situation can be formulated as follows: Not only those who were called to obedience in the Church, but also those who were quite ready to give it, found that the exercise of authority in the Church in part no longer corresponded to the time and was no longer tolerable. In the face of continuous and insistent appeals to obedience and "childlike trust" of the ecclesiastical authority, one had the impression that commands did not take account of the urgent needs and tasks of the Church, that irrelevant views predominated, and that, when it came to a decisive point, the authorities were not prepared to face the issues properly or to allow new views to be discussed. The problem became a choice between readiness to obey the Church and an understanding of urgent needs in the Church's life and in theology. It is enough to point out that the conciliar decrees as well as those matters with which a large majority in the Council were concerned tended in directions which were rejected in high—even the highest—places, although one should not think that this whole new orientation came about only since 1962.

This development provided also the way in which the problem of authority was formulated. On the one hand, there was the non-hierarchical section of the Church where a growing religious, theological and ecclesiastical revival led to an increase in interest, participation and factual competence in matters of the Church—and this is in harmony with the New Testament image of the Church and with theology.[9] On the other hand, there was the hierarchical section where an absolutist attitude continued

[8] Cf. *ibid.*, pp. 22-48.
[9] Cf. *ibid.*, pp. 62-3; 84-5; 98-106; 251-3.

to operate, which did not correspond to the theological reality of the Church.

Looking back to this pre-conciliar period which has not yet been completely overcome, we may therefore indicate the following points in connection with the problem of authority.

There is no longer any room for absolutism in the Church. By this we mean that kind of "overlordship" which proceeds as an exclusive monologue; where the authority merely decrees without genuinely listening to those to whom the orders are given; where justice is limited to the pronouncement of ready-made judgments and the person concerned is deprived of any legal remedy; where even questions of theology are "governed" by command and prohibition although this is a contradiction in terms; where the members of the loving community of the body of Christ, even when their disposition cannot be questioned, live in an atmosphere of fear which would suit a police state. When, in such a whole situation, the authority lays claim even to the conscience of the "subject", we have a clear case of totalitarianism, and the Church of Christ will be identified with other totalitarian systems, whether she likes it or not.

As a form of government, absolutism is a contradiction of the Church's nature. In the Church, indeed, there is no such sharp division between "ruler" and "subject". Every member of the Church participates in Christ, in his priesthood, his prophetic function and his kingship. If, in virtue of Christ's foundation, there are official functions and people without such an official function in the Church's structure, this distinction exists only within the perspective of the community as a whole, the equal and undifferentiated basis of all members of Christ.

It therefore does not correspond to the reality of the Church to exaggerate the phenomenon of obedience in general, and to create the impression that the highest and only Christian task of the member without official function is merely to obey the hierarchy. This obedience has its place, but this place is neither the only one nor the principal feature of the Church's life.

(B) Therefore, we can now trace the main lines on which the

problem of authority should develop in the new epoch of the Church.

1. When authority is mentioned in the Church, it should always refer first of all and essentially to Christ's authority. Christ has not simply "bequeathed" his authority to the hierarchy. The glorified Lord rules his Church directly and permanently. His word is obligatory always and for all; he distributes the prompting of his spirit as he wills. The hierarchy represents Christ's authority and makes it present, but this authority of Christ does not simply belong to them. It is a theological question of infallibility and of concrete judgment, whether or not the full authority of Christ is vouched for in any given utterance by the hierarchy. It cannot be a *claim* of the Church's authorities that their authority must always be identified with that of Christ; rather, it is their duty to *try* to represent Christ's authority as much as possible in their acts of government. This is the basis of the credibility of their function.

2. This is what Christ meant when he said to his disciples: "But you are not to be called rabbi, for you have one teacher, and you are all brethren. And call no man your father on earth, for you have one Father, who is in heaven. Neither be called masters, for you have one master, the Christ. He who is greatest among you shall be your servant" (Matt. 23, 8-11). Ecclesiastical authority is in essence fraternal authority. It does not create an essential division of superiority and subordination; it is among brothers, and all are equally and essentially under the authority of the Father, the master, the teacher. This should not be a mere figure of speech, but must be reflected in the reality of the Church's life. The quotation of Christ just mentioned should be appealed to in the Church just as frequently as Matthew 16, 18, where for too long and because of historical factors the Roman and Germanic image of the authority of the father, the tribe and the prince has competed with the image of authority in the Gospel.

It is this image of the Gospel which sets the right tone for obedience and authority in the life of the Church. To command in the Church means to bear responsibility for what is the good of all, for what corresponds to the deepest will of the living members and springs from the common and conscious concern of all the members who are ready to cooperate. These members will then recognize the special place of the guide and pastor without further ado. Instead of being taken by surprise at a new command, the member without official function should see in it the fruit of common understanding, common concern and common responsibility. Only then does such a command fit into its rightful function.

3. Everyone talks about "unrest" in the Church. Everything is moving. The stability of authority is not only shattered in practice but has also become uncertain in theory. That this situation contains "dangers" hardly needs to be stressed. There are dangers in every imaginable human situation, and the dangers of the former situation have already been outlined. But there is here also a promise, an appeal. The situation of the Church is certainly not saved by an overly clever and infallible functioning of a system of administration, but only by the presence of the glorified Lord, just as the support of teaching is not saved by an incontrovertible theological system, but only through the working of the Holy Spirit. The period of unrest should be used as a call of grace to everyone to put his whole trust for the Church genuinely in the Lord and his spirit. It may well be a grace in itself by which we are undeceived of a former deception.

There nevertheless remain many practical problems of concrete ecclesiastical government, of an unseemly loss of orderliness. Here the pastors need the right type of intelligent guidance. When the laity and clergy of a Church want to go ahead in the dazzle of unexpected new perspectives but have not yet found the correct procedure, they should not be stopped by warning against all the "new dangers", or by stressing above all what remains "forbidden in spite of everything", or by creating the impression that the pastors only reluctantly follow the movement of the whole Church and would rather make it come to a halt again.

This would lead to a new mistrust, by which the last things would really be worse than the first.

However, when a pastor makes it clear that he identifies himself with the movement of the Church, and even cares to lead the way as guide, using the bridle only in order to encourage, then he will find that he has the support of convinced followers. Then a word of restraint will be accepted, since it will not rouse any suspicions, and he will find loyal support when he has to fight excesses that are genuinely damaging.

This is the problem of authority and obedience in the Church at the present hour.

Alonzo-M. Hamelin, O.F.M./*Montreal, Canada*

Man's Rights over His Body and the Principle of Totality

Every day the progress of science poses new problems for the theologian. How far, for example, do man's rights over his body extend? Revelation makes the human creature subject to the sovereign authority of God. Yet, Christian charity demands that man sacrifice himself for the good of others. Does not the Gospel state that there is no greater love than to lay down one's life for one's friend? Earlier ages were marked by individualism, but our modern world has discovered the social dimension of humanity. Men wish to meet each other, to get to know each other; they are becoming aware of their solidarity. But we also recognize that the pressure of social groups on the individual may not take sufficient account of human dignity and liberty.

Theologians have often had recourse to the principle of totality to try to discover how far a man may sacrifice himself for the good of the community. This principle "asserts that the part exists for the whole and that, consequently, the good of the part remains subordinate to the good of the whole; that the whole is a determining factor for the part and can dispose of it in its own interest".[1]

[1] Pius XII, "Alloc. au Cong. d'Histopathologie," Sept. 13, 1952, in *A.S.S.* 44 (1952), p. 788. We have used the translation from *The Major Addresses of Pope Pius XII*, ed. Vincent A. Yzermans, I (St. Paul, 1961), p. 233. J. Madiran quotes a series of texts from Aristotle and St. Thomas confirming the teachings of Pius XII in his *Le principe de totalité* (Nouvelles Edit. Latines, 1962), pp. 12-4. St. Bonaventure and the Scholastics repeat the same ideas.

It is an immutable principle, certainly, for it "flows from the essence of ideas and things", but it is not so easy to apply in practice. The principle applies only "where the relationship of a whole to its part holds good, and in the exact measure that it holds good".[2] And God knows that it is not always easy to verify the extent of the subordination of the part to the whole.

Furthermore, we must admit that the very notion of subordination is liable to vary. First of all, we know how philosophers and theologians, as well as jurists, tend to develop their principles on the basis of facts. The application of principles always depends therefore on one's concept of man, and this partial and modifiable concept brings with it variable applications. Finally, we are all aware of the Church's constant care for the dignity of man, a care that leads her to adapt, to expound, and sometimes even to defend her authentic doctrine according to the requirements of the evolution of man and of society. There is a case, then, for a further study of the principle of totality, in a wide context that will reveal its wide possibilities.[3]

From the very beginning, this principle has been applied most obviously on the level of the physical organism, in which all the parts are substantially united to the whole. This application serves as a prototype in studying the ontological relations ruling social bodies, and even the most complete organism, the human race. While recognizing the personal dignity of the human being, we shall try to elucidate the bonds that unite him to all men and make him the cell of a living organism in time and space. Therefore our study falls naturally into two parts.

[2] *Ibid.*

[3] Recently several authors have written on the principle of totality. Among them we frequently refer to G. Kelly, "Pope Pius XII and the Principle of Totality," in *Theol. Stud.* 16 (1955), pp. 373-96; J. Madiran, *op. cit.;* M. Nolan, "The Positive Doctrine of Pope Pius XII on the Principle of Totality," in *Augustinianum,* 3 (1963), pp. 28-44; 290-324.

I

THE HUMAN ORGANISM

The first applications of the principle of totality regard the organism as a substantial unity: the human body. Without delaying to give the philosophical definitions of the terms "whole" and "part" [4] we shall turn immediately to the study of their reciprocal relationships.

In keeping with the medical knowledge of his time, Pius XI made a restrictive application of this principle to mutilation "when no other provision can be made for the good of the whole body".[5] Besides, this is the only application which the ancients knew. Pius XI quotes St. Thomas,[6] but all authors are unanimous on this point and the most popular moralists of the 14th and 15th centuries, Astésanus[7] and Angelus Carletti de Clavasio,[8] summarize the doctrine prevalent at that time.

Pius XII's presentation is, however, more positive. Man "can also intervene as often as and to the extent that the good of the whole demands, to destroy, mutilate and separate the members".[9] Man's right of disposal of his body is now more extensive and even offers possibilities capable of being varied according to the interpretation of the terms.

The first thing to note is that the Pope speaks of the "good of the whole". While it is true that Pius XII uses the term "orga-

[4] In reference to this point, cf. M. Nolan, *op. cit.*, pp. 23ff.

[5] *Casti Connubii, A.A.S.* 22 (1930), p. 565. We have used the translation of the National Catholic Welfare Conference, *Christian Marriage* (Washington, D.C., 1931), p. 24.

[6] *Summa Theol.* II, II, q. 108, a. 4.

[7] *Summ. Astensis, lib. 1, tit. 26, ad 1,* I (Edit. Romae, 1728), p. 87: "It is also permitted for a private person of his own volition, whose member is in question, or for the person who has legal responsibility for him, to cut off a diseased member for the purpose of preserving his bodily health; but otherwise, it is never permissible."

[8] *Summ. Angelica, ad verbum "Homicidium" I ad 2,* I (Edit. Venitiis, 1582), p. 586: "Is it permissible for anyone to kill or mutilate himself? I answer, not without mortal sin, because no one is master of his members. But this does not apply to mutilation for the sake of health; it is then permitted."

[9] *Op. cit.*, p. 232.

nism", theologians of today agree in understanding "the good of the whole" to mean not only the good of the physical organism, but also the good of the whole person.[10] Now the total good of the person is the good of "the psychosomatic unity insofar as it is determined and governed by the human soul".[11] It is, therefore, completely plausible to admit that the parts are in substantial relation with the spiritual finality of man, as well as and even more than with his natural finality. The Pope expresses himself in this sense in at least one of his allocutions.[12] The scriptural texts in which Christ demands the sacrifice of the physical members to assure entrance into the kingdom of heaven[13] are not then to be taken solely in a spiritual sense. If they show how energetically we must pursue evil even to its roots, they also affirm a definite right for a man to sacrifice a part of his body for the good of his soul. Is it not this that justifies the dangers freely accepted in the mission field or in mortifications? Again, such a mutilation must be as necessary as a surgical operation.

This introduces the second point to be elucidated, namely, the relationship of necessity that must exist between the act posited and the end desired. Christian tradition has always interpreted the evangelical texts in the figurative sense, because it did not see any necessity for positing these acts.[14] True enough. But could they not sometimes be really useful? Here again, in spite of the

[10] Cf. M. Nolan, op. cit., pp. 295-301; G. Kelly, op. cit., p. 379. The expression seems to have been popularized by J. Connery, "Notes on Moral Theology," in Theol. Stud. 15 (1954), p. 602.

[11] Pius XII, "Alloc. au Congr. de la Société Intern. de la Psychologie appliquée," April 10, 1958, in A.A.S. 50 (1958), p. 269.

[12] For example: "Alloc. au Congr. du Coll. Intern. de Neuro-Psycho-Pharmatologie," Sept. 9, 1958, in A.S.S. 50 (1958), pp. 693-94: "While particular organs must be subordinated to the organism and to its end, the organism itself must be subordinated to the spiritual end of the person."

[13] Matt. 5, 29: "If your right eye tempts you to sin, pluck it out and throw it away; it is better for you that one of your members should perish than that, body and all, you should be thrown into the eternal pit," Kleist-Lilly, The New Testament (Milwaukee, 1956). See also Mark 9, 43-47.

[14] Cf. Summ. Astensis, loc. cit.: "In no case is it permitted to cut off a member for the sake of avoiding sin. It is always possible to promote one's spiritual welfare by means other than cutting off a member, since sin is subject to the will."

fact that Pius XII most frequently expresses himself in terms of necessity, scholars understand him in the wider meaning of usefulness or convenience. It is not always easy to draw the line of demarcation between necessity and utility.[15]

With these points established, it is possible to resolve the medical problems of lobotomy, electric-shock therapy, and so forth,[16] according to the principle of totality. Mutilation to escape death, or sterilization under pain of being excluded from society can also be justified on the same grounds.[17] Certain cases of sterilization of women require more attention. If the organs themselves are affected with serious ailments involving grave consequences, their total removal is readily permitted. But when the danger results only from a new pregnancy, Pius XII leaves it clearly understood that the principle of totality does not apply since it is sufficient merely to stop using the organ.[18]

The problem, however, can take on another aspect. An opinion has become prevalent today which Father O'Donnell justifies as follows: "Since an organ is essentially called to a special function, one cannot say that it is or is not pathological except in relationship to its function." [19] The removal of a uterus damaged by multiple Caesarian sections, for example, seems, then, to be fully justifiable. Father Tesson has shown the extensions of such an application. If one approves hysterectomy, why not accept also the tying off of the Fallopian tubes under the same circumstances? We can go even further in a similar *a fortiori* argument: we do not find it more difficult to accept the practice of using chemical

[15] G. Kelly, "Notes on Moral Theology," in *Theol. Stud.* 9 (1948), pp. 93-4; cf. also his "Pope Pius XII . . ." pp. 379-82; and Regatillo-Zalba, *Theologia Moralis Summa* II (Madrid, 1953), n. 251.

[16] Cf. G. Kelly, "The Morality of Mutilation," in *Theol. Stud.* 17 (1956), pp. 334-44. We mention this author because he seems to have best synthesized this question of casuistry.

[17] Cf. G. Kelly, "Notes on Moral Theology," *loc. cit.* 15 (1954), pp. 605-6; also his "Pope Pius XII . . ." *loc. cit.* 16 (1955), pp. 383-5, and "The Morality of Mutilation," *loc. cit.* p. 336.

[18] Cf. G. Kelly, "Notes on Moral Theology," in *Theol. Stud.* 12 (1951), pp. 70-1.

[19] *La morale en médecine,* Coll. Siècle et Catholicisme (Paris, ²1962), p. 153.

substances to arrest ovulation[20] on condition, however, that these compounds have no harmful effect on the organism as a whole.[21] And still arguing from the principle of totality, neither do we see any reasons that would prevent extending the application to all those pathological cases in which the life of the mother is imperilled by a new pregnancy. We personally believe that this conclusion is acceptable.

Until now we have limited ourselves to considering pathological situations. Can preventive action also claim the same justification? Indeed, there seems to be no clear case for restricting the principle to diseased organs.[22] We could not now blame a woman for taking advance precautions against a possible pregnancy—by taking pills preventing ovluation—if she foresees that she risks being violated, for example, during a time of social troubles.[23] But what can we say when these medicines are taken for the purpose of safeguarding family values?

Before answering this question, let us emphasize the reasons that justify applying the principle of totality to the human body. The organs of the human body are constitutive parts of its physical being and have no reason for existence outside of the physical organism.[24] Once this well-defined relationship has been stated, it is sufficient to indicate the two terms of the relationship, that is, the corporeal organs, diseased or not, and the total good of the person in question. But in the social organism, the relationship of the parts to the whole requires other clarifications. Let us try to elucidate this social aspect.

[20] Cf. E. Tesson, "Discussion morale," in *Cahiers Laennec*, 24 (June, 1964), pp. 69-71.
[21] Cf. J. Ferin, "De l'utilisation des médicaments 'inhibiteurs d'ovulation,'" in *Eph. Theol. Lov.* 39 (1963), pp. 779-86.
[22] Pope Pius XII, "Alloc. au congr. d'Urologie," Oct. 8, 1953, in *A.A.S.* 45 (1953), p. 674; cf. also G. Kelly, *Medico-Moral Problems* (St. Louis, 1948), p. 28.
[23] Cf. E. Tesson, *op. cit.*, p. 72.
[24] Cf. Pope Pius XII, "Alloc. à l'union médico-biologique St-Luc," Nov. 12, 1944; also his "Alloc. au Congr. d'Histopathologie," Sept. 13, 1952, *loc. cit.*, p. 786.

II

THE SOCIAL ORGANISM

Philosophers and theologians have always considered the primacy of the common good when referring to the principle of totality. "A particular good," said St. Thomas, "is ordered to the common good as to an end; indeed, the being of a part depends on the being of the whole. So, also, the good of a nation is more godlike than the good of one man." [25] This means, however, that the whole noetic system of the universe still revolves around the human person, "foundation, cause and end of all social institutions".[26]

René Coste has produced a succinct and comprehensive summary of the dignity of the human person and his call to live in universal brotherhood and in a supernatural organism, the mystical body of Christ.[27] St. Bonaventure's view of society strengthens the bonds of human solidarity still further. Society is best manifested in the totality of universal unification. As the living body harmonizes the different vital energies and shows a perfect synthesis of tendencies, so does the social body. Society is a dynamic order in which the social being tends to the most perfect realization of its end. Thus it is essentially hierarchical, in the sense that it necessarily involves a sort of linking of beings and their actions. Strictly speaking, the hierarchy relates to God, the unique principle of being and of its operation. There is interdependence among men united voluntarily in this social order, so that each one depends necessarily on his neighbor whom he needs for the realization of his personal end. Thus in the human world there is established a constitution based not only on feeling but also on

[25] *Summa Contra Gentiles, lib. III, cap. xvii.* Our translation is from Vernon P. Bourke, *On the Truth of the Catholic Faith* (New York, 1956), p. 72. For a study of parallel sources, see F. Utz, *Ethique social* I (Fribourg, 1960), *Appendix,* in which the author reproduces the work of A. Verpaalen; cf. also R. Jaquin, "Individu et société d'après saint Thomas," in *Rev. Sc. Relig.* 35 (1961), pp. 183-90.

[26] John XXIII, *Mater et Magistra,* in *A.A.S.* 53 (1961), p. 451.

[27] *Morale internationale,* Coll. Bibl. de Théologie, Section Morale (Paris: Desclée et Cie, 1964), pp. 101-22.

charity.[28] For St. Bonaventure, society is a sort of vital coordination of spiritual and temporal elements, as is the case in the living body of man where all energies, spiritual and material, are put into operation only in view of the common good of the human person.

We must not conclude from this that all the possible applications of the principle of totality to the human body can be taken over entirely into a social context and used here. By entering into society, a man does not lose his quality of person, which is not only outside the collective value, but infinitely beyond it. This is not to justify the Aristotelian opposition: if man is a substantial being, society is something more than the purely accidental, and requires an active collaboration from the individual.[29]

Two conclusions spring from these considerations. First, the State does not have the same authority over its members as man has over his own body. As Pius XII said, "Considered as a whole, the community is not a physical unity subsisting in itself, and its individual members are not integral parts of it." [30] A social group is a community of persons each of whom has his dignity and deserves respect. Authority, then, does not have absolute power over its subjects.

On the other hand, we must admit that the individual person can best and most easily attain his full development within the common good. From this it follows that he not only can, but in certain circumstances must, subordinate his actions to the benefit of the group, and this subordination can go as far as the sacrifice of his own life. And it is here, in our opinion, that State inter-

[28] We have tried to give, as succinctly as possible, St. Bonaventure's concept of society. It does not seem practical or necessary to indicate all the references we have used. For a more extensive study, see H. Legowicz, *Essai sur la philosophie sociale du Docteur séraphique* (Fribourg, 1938), pp. 140-60; also M. de Benedictis, *The Social Thought of St. Bonaventure* (Washington, 1946).

[29] The reciprocal ordering of the person and society has often been studied. Cf., for example, C. de Konink, *De la primauté du bien commun* (Montréal, 1943); J. Maritain, *La personne et le bien commun* (Paris: Desclée de Brouwer, 1947); also J. Madiran, *op. cit.,* pp. 51-84.

[30] "Alloc. au Congr. d'Histopathologie," *loc. cit.,* p. 232.

vention comes in. It is to man personally that the prudent use of his body is confided; but, where this obligation is indicated, public authority can intervene and demand that the individual carry out his social duty. In other cases, the State has only the alternative of inviting his cooperation. The vitality of the group is primordial only on the condition that it is envisioned from the standpoint of its real values.

In this line of thought, it is a question of man first, then of society, the latter becoming for man the means of realizing his own finality. For, in order to reach this finality, man must travel via the common good, and the common good cannot be accomplished without some limitation of individual rights, without the individual having the choice of disposing of himself in the interests of the group. Charity makes him take cognizance of his solidarity with other men; it makes him available for the sacrifice demanded for the good of all. It is in this sense that life in society leads the human person to his perfection. Through the common good, man must know how to recognize and pursue the true good of his own personality, as St. Bonaventure teaches.[31] Let us say, then, that the profit to be drawn is, definitively, in the interests of the part, but this profit is realizable only by passing through the whole. And this is another difference of application of the principle of totality to the human organism, whose sole finality is achieved in the whole at the expense of the part. Seeing the question in this light, we cannot admit the exaggerated concept of the State's power which the ancient philosophers held,[32] any more than the exaggerated claims of certain totalitarian States today of absolute power over their subjects.[33] Nor can we, on the other hand, condemn man's initiative to sacrifice himself for the sake of the community. The domain of experimentation is a case in point. A narrow interpretation of the principle of totality recognizes

[31] Cf. *Coll. de Donis Spiritus S.*, IV, n. 10, V (Edit. Quaracchi, 1892-1901), p. 475b.

[32] For example, Aristotle, *Politics*, VIII, 1.

[33] Cf. J. Madiran, *op. cit.* His whole book is concerned with refuting the errors of totalitarianism. He quotes numerous texts of the magisterium.

as legitimate only the case in which the patient, already ill, sees in the use of an experimental drug his only chance of recovery.[34] Present-day theologians are less severe. For an experiment to be licit, they require the free consent of the subject, a high probability of success, and care in taking all recommended precautions.[35] This attitude seems to be quite in accordance with the true norms of the principle of totality: respect for the person and the seeking of a common good to the definite benefit of the individual. Certainly some risk remains, but a prudent usage of the goods that God has placed in our hands does not exclude all risk. Anyone who travels nowadays runs serious and constant risks. And who would wish to condemn the astronauts for the risks they take for the progress of humanity?[36] Medical experiments would seem to be merely a particular application of a common principle.

The case of the transplantation of human organs offers another practical application. The question is this: Can a person, because of human solidarity and through his membership in the mystical body, at least by vocation, consent to be mutilated for the welfare of another? This is the view taken by Fr. Cunningham, S.J., a few years ago.[37] Theologians were reluctant to accept it at first, but gradually, and after a few tergiversations on the part of some of them, many have brought themselves to accept it, although not arguing from the principle of totality.[38] We wonder why. Father

[34] The common doctrine still holds to this point of view. Cf. *Ami du Clergé* 57 (1947), p. 679; also J. Paquin, *Morale et médecine* (Montréal, 1955), pp. 239-42.

[35] Cf. P. Cruchon, "Expérimentation sur l'homme dans le domaine corporel et dans le domaine psychologique," in *Perspectives et limites de l'expérimentation sur l'homme* (Paris, 1960), pp. 65-89; G. Kelly, "Pope Pius XII . . ." *op. cit.*, pp. 385-91; E. Tesson, "Réflexions morales," in *Cahiers Laennec*, 12 (June, 1952), pp. 27-39.

[36] For the good of the community we must constantly run risks of all sorts. Cf. J. Lynch, "Notes on Moral Theology," in *Theol. Stud.* 17 (1956), pp. 174-6.

[37] B. Cunningham, *The Morality of Organic Transplantation* (Washington, D.C., 1944).

[38] Father Cunningham's book has stirred up a rather lively controversy; it would be pretentious to try to give all the positions taken and to indicate all the writings provoked by his thesis. Let us indicate three characteristic positions: (a) *Those decidedly unfavorable:* P. Hurth, Prof.

Kelly has often put forward the argument that charity is the basis of the moral value of such an operation; Father Connell likewise. But it is just this same charity that unites an individual to the community and to each member of the community. Basically, what bothers present-day theologians is that Christian tradition has always regarded mutilation as intrinsically evil.[39] On the basis of the

at the Gregorianum (Rome), at least in his oral discourses (cf. G. Kelly, "Notes on Moral Theology," in *Theol. Stud.* 24 (1963), pp. 627-30; F. Iorio, *Theologia Moralis* II (Naples, 1939), n. 200; Noldin-Schmitt-Heinzel, *Summa Theol. Moralis* II (Innsbruck, 1954), n. 328; L. Bender, "Organorum humanorum transplantatio," in *Angelicum* 31 (1954), pp. 139-60; J. Wroe, *Catholic Medical Quarterly* 16 (1963), pp. 61ff; and others; (b) *Favorable, but with reservations:* Regatillo-Zalba, *op. cit.,* p. 268. After having clearly taken up a position against Father Cunningham, Father Zalba changed his mind, and while maintaining the essentials of his own thesis, recognized, however, an extrinsic probability in the contrary thesis: "La mutilacion y el transplanto de organos a la luz del magisterio eclesiastico," in *Razón y Fe* 153 (1956), pp. 523-48; J. Geraud, "Peut-on donner un oeil à un aveugle?" in *Ami du Clergé* 65 (1955), p. 167; J. Paquin, *op. cit.,* p. 247; (c) *Clearly favorable, with only a few reservations regarding proofs:* G. Kelly, in several of his "Notes on Moral Theology," published in *Theol. Stud.* from 1947 to the present. There we can follow the evolution of his thought and the statement of his convictions. Two articles especially mark the synthesis of his thought: "Pope Pius XII and . . ." *op. cit.,* pp. 391-96, and "The Morality of Mutilation," *op. cit.,* pp. 322-44; J. McCarthy, "The Morality of Organic Transplantation," in *Irish Eccl. Record* 67 (1946), pp. 192-98; L. Babbini, "Moralità del trapianto di un membro pari," in *Palestra del Clero* 34 (1955), pp. 359-61; F. Connell, "The Pope's Teaching on Organic Transplantation," in *Am. Eccl. Rev.* 135 (1956), pp. 159-70; E. Tesson, "Greffe humaine et morale," in *Cahiers Laennec* 16 (March, 1956), pp. 28-33; J. Snock, "Transplantaçao organica entre vivos humanos," in *Rev. Ecl. Brasileira* 19 (1959), pp. 785-95; G. Healy, "Medical Ethics," in *Philippine Studies* 7 (1959), pp. 461-79; T. O'Donnell, *op. cit.,* pp. 131-33.

[39] Some authors' manner of procedure is a bit curious. Cf., for example, J. McCarthy, *op. cit.,* p. 198; G. Kelly, "Pope Pius XII and . . ." pp. 392-96; and his "The Morality of Mutilation," *loc. cit.,* pp. 322-344, especially p. 342; and J. Connery, "Notes on Moral Theology," in *Theol. Stud.* 15 (1954), pp. 603-4. These authors let it be understood that either an evil can be permitted for a proportionate cause—which is not at all acceptable in the present teaching of the Church—or that mutilation is not intrinsically evil—which goes counter to another tradition, less well established, however, than one might think. We prefer this second hypothesis. Furthermore, in our opinion, this is the difficulty that restrained Pius XII from applying the principle of totality to organic transplantation. Cf. "Alloc. aux Ophthalmologistes," May 14, 1956, in *A.A.S.* 48 (1956), p. 461.

fact that God is master of life, the conclusion has always been drawn that he is equally the sovereign master of all corporeal organs.

God is master of life, certainly, but he gives this life to man to enjoy and by that very fact leaves it in his hands for him to *use it prudently.*[40] Now prudent usage supposes a certain initiative and a justifiable authority on the part of man. The usufructuary enjoys the usage of a thing as though it belonged to him, on the condition, however, that he preserve its substance. The duty of preserving his life is incumbent on man in strict justice, but his acts of usage are contingent. To cut off an arm in the case of necessity is as much an act of prudent usage as filling one's stomach when one is hungry. In the case of organic transplantation, the principles of human solidarity and fraternal charity indicate the lines of prudent usage without having to render good what would be intrinsically evil.

And so, finally, does the social unit of the family permit a legitimate application of the principle of totality? Social charity orientates man toward society as a whole; the same tendency urges him toward another person and leads him to contract marriage. In this relationship he takes a first step toward the inter-personal union favorable not only to the birth and rearing of a child, but also to the personal development of each of the spouses through the reciprocal complement that they bring to each other. St. Bonaventure shows, here again, how the two ends of marriage are obtained by the same means: the reciprocal love of spouses created in the image of God.[41] Marriage is first of all a real society, a union of reasonable beings whose unifying principle is love.

---

[40] Father O'Donnell frequently returns to the question of wise administration, *op. cit.,* pp. 63-4, 125-6, and other passages. It seems to us, however, that he does not give the full force of conviction to this argument which, to us seems to be of prime importance. Cf. M. Nolan, *op. cit.,* pp. 309-12.

[41] *I Sent. dist. 10, art. 2, q. 1.* "Husband and wife love each other with a social love for the purpose of living together and with a conjugal love for the procreation of children." Unfortunately, this aspect of marriage has never been sufficiently elucidated in St. Bonaventure. However, cf. H. Legowicz, *op. cit.,* pp. 161-82.

Husbands and wives, as members of a family, have rights insofar as they are persons; but, as members of a society, they also have duties. Their activity must be orientated toward the common good of the family, even at the price of some individual sacrifices. Unfortunately, this limitation is too often forgotten. For example, when discussing the emancipation of woman, we think of assuring her the utmost liberty; but do we remind her with equal force that, insofar as she is part of a whole, she must sacrifice her personal choice to the good of the whole, that is, to the good of her family?

The same spirit of solidarity makes it praiseworthy for a mother to risk an operation for the good of the child she is bearing. Why, on the same grounds, could not the married couple accept, or even seek, a temporary mutilation for the greater good of family life? Evidently, there is no question of justifying personal egoism, but of benefiting the common good. We do not wish to insist on the casuistry consequent upon the principle of totality; but this last certainly opens perspectives on a problem which is currently of great concern to us: that of birth control.

Therefore, the principle of totality, properly understood, has many possible applications in the realm of man's rights over his body. Although in the past Christian morality in practice reserved these applications to the physical organism, we can, it seems, use them far more widely: in any case, in fact, involving the relationship of the part to the whole and to the degree in which these relationships obtain. This is not to say that we are deceiving ourselves about its inherent dangers and possible abuses.

It also seems particularly important to clarify another point: it is not the principle of totality in itself that licenses these acts in which the individual exercises his rights over his body. It is only a criterion assuring man's prudent usage of the goods entrusted to him by the Creator. Human goods, let us not forget, are made for man's use; man himself is created for God.

PART II

BIBLIOGRAPHICAL SURVEY

Theodore L. Westow/*Salisbury, England*

The Argument about Pacifism: A Critical Survey of English Studies

I n England there are over 50 different organizations directly concerned with peace; in the United
States there are at least 35. On the Continent there seem to be
16 in Germany, 13 in France, 10 in Italy, 11 in the Netherlands
and 8 in Belgium. Most of the English-speaking organizations
have their own publications. This may be due to the Anglo-
Saxon preference for concrete problems, and, consequently, for
Christian realities rather than theories. On the other hand, both
the United States and England are already in possession of a vast
nuclear war machinery which throttles the national economy. Not
only the taxpayer (England spends well over £2,000,000,000
per year on "defense"), but also the Army, the Navy and
Air Force, the scientist, the industrialist, the factory-worker,
the businessman and the educator—all are involved in a situation that considers war as the only practical issue and peace as
an impossible ideal. This lack of balance in itself is enough to
provoke determined resistance in a live democracy. Anglo-Saxon
Christians are therefore bound to ask themselves sooner or later
whether Christianity is relevant in this situation.

The material is so vast that it would require several volumes
to embrace it all. It therefore seemed sensible to present this
survey as an argument, proceeding from the surface to the heart
of the matter, and to refer only to those studies which make a

real contribution to the argument. The published material could easily fill a library,[1] and since there is inevitably much repetition, some animosity and a fair amount of superficial discussion which might confuse the issue, selection is the only possible solution.

For the same reasons "pacifism" is here limited to the rejection of war, and "war" to armed conflict between nations or groups of nations. I am not concerned here with any other brand of "peace" or any other brand of "war".

To obtain a quick and objective idea of what is implied in nuclear war, Tom Stonier's *Nuclear Disaster*[2] will be most useful. This can be followed up by the history of the Pugwash Conferences, published by Prof. J. Rotblat.[3] At the first Conference (1957) it was stated: "It is our conviction that the paramount responsibility of scientists is to do all in their power to prevent war and to help establish a permanent and universal peace." [4] I quote this statement, not because of its generalities, but because it shows that these scientists do *not* treat the problem as an academic issue but as human beings who are *personally* involved in the matter. It is precisely a common complaint of the pacifists that theologians rarely take this attitude, that they deal with the problem as if it were merely a very difficult case to be solved according to the textbook.

Studies on the psychological, sociological and anthropological aspects of war have been conveniently put together by L. Bramson and G. W. Goethals;[5] such studies, again, practically never

[1] For instance, the library of the International Fellowship of Reconciliation in London. Here I wish to express my gratitude to the Rev. E. P. Eastman, Secretary of the International Fellowship, for his generous assistance; to Mr. Donald Groom for introducing me to him and to the library of the Society of Friends; to Mr. Walter Stein, of the University of Leeds, for his jovial encouragement; and to Mr. Justus George Lawler for allowing me to have a preview of his book, *Nuclear War*.

[2] T. Stonier, *Nuclear Disaster* (World Pub. Co., 1963), in which there are 18 pages of bibliography. For the political and strategic reality of the problem, the basic works are by H. Kahn: *The Thermonuclear War* (Princeton, 1960), and *On Escalation* (New York: Pall Mall, 1965).

[3] J. Rotblat, *Science and World Affairs* (London, 1962).

[4] *Ibid.*, p. 47.

[5] *War. Studies from Psychology, Sociology and Anthropology* (ed. by L. Bramson and G. Goethals) (New York/London, 1964). This book contains a selective bibliography on pp. 395-7.

appear in any manual of moral theology on this point. Particularly interesting is the study by Margaret Mead, "Warfare Is Only an Invention—Not a Biological Necessity," [6] the title of which is sufficiently clear to need no further explanation.

Two major studies appeared which put the whole discussion into a proper historical perspective. Dr. R. H. Bainton's work on *Christian Attitudes toward War and Peace,*[7] very readable and containing much fascinating material, leads him in the end to the pacifist side of the argument, and his charm is very persuasive. The other study is by G. S. Windass.[8] This work, essential for any student of this problem, is more a history of the theological side of the argument. Beginning with the Christian protest of the early Church, the author leads the argument on to the period of "accommodation", then to the "consecration of violence" in the Middle Ages, at the end of which the "protest" is "humanized", only to be followed by the systematic "accommodation" through the influence of Vittoria and Suarez, so as to celebrate the rise of the Nation-State. From this point on, the "world" takes over and the author finishes with a very relevant discussion on "inappropriate" and "appropriate attitudes" toward the problem today. The whole is written with much fairness and the style is gentle; the final appeal is to a genuine "Christian" fellowship.

At this point we come to a flood of studies which circle more or less around the "theory" of the "just war". It seems proper to start with the official declarations of the Churches.[9] The real

[6] *Ibid.,* pp. 269-74.

[7] London, 1960.

[8] G. Windass, *Christianity versus Violence* (London, 1964).

[9] *The Voice of the Church concerning Modern War* (London: The Friends Peace Committee [Quakers], 1963); the *Report of the Oxford Conference in 1937,* and that of the *Amsterdam Conference of the World Council of Churches in 1948.* The W.C.C. also sponsored *Christians and the Prevention of War in an Atomic Age* (London: S.C.M. Press, 1961). The British Council of Churches published a report on *The Era of Atomic Power* (London: S.P.C.K., 1946). The same year saw the publication of *Atomic Warfare and the Christian Faith* by the American National Council of Churches. The British Council of Churches then published *Christians and Atomic War* (1959) and *The Valley of Decision* (1961), written by T. Milford. The Church of England brought out *The Church and*

background of all these documents is found in the reports of the
Oxford Conference in 1937 and that of Amsterdam in 1948. The
opening statement was: "We are one in proclaiming to all mankind: War is contrary to the will of God." This was a plain theological statement, but after this statement the argument shilly-
shallied till the conclusion was reached at Amsterdam that it is
the Christian's "duty to defend law by force if necessary".[10] The
confusion arose from the difficulty of reconciling an "uncompromising obedience to a kingdom not of this world" with "the no
less insistent Christian responsibility to defend the fundamental
rights and liberties of men and the institutions through which
in our society these are affirmed, protected and developed".[11]
But what exactly is meant by "our society"? Which institutions
must be defended? And most disturbing of all questions: Why
must these be defended by military force? This kind of sentence
hardly conceals the ambiguity of the argument and is unfortunately typical of all the documents. It is therefore refreshing to
meet the frank statement by Sir Thomas Taylor and Robert S.
Bilheimer at the end of their report to the World Council of
Churches: "We frankly admit, however, that we do not see how
the requirements of the Gospel can be made relevant to the dangerous situation of the present time, save in terms which limit
objectives in this fashion." [12] It is also admitted that the theory

---

the Atom in 1948 and *Modern War: What Can Christians Do Together?*
in 1962 (led by the Bishop of Leicester). *The Christian and War* (Lon-
don, 1958) contains *Peace Is the Will of God,* a statement by the His-
toric Peace Churches to the World Council in 1953; *God Wills Both*
Justice and Peace by Bishop Dunn and R. Niebuhr (first published in
Christianity and Crisis XV, n. 10, 1955) and a reply by the European
Continuation Committee of the Historic Peace Churches: *God Establishes*
Both Peace and Justice. In the same way, a group of pacifists, led by
G. Fawcett, published a reply to *The Valley of Decision* in *The Uphill*
Way, on behalf of the Friends (London: Friends House, 1962). Lastly,
there is *The British Nuclear Deterrent,* published by the British Council
of Churches in 1963, which contains the report of a Working Group led
by Kenneth Johnstone.

[10] *The Christian and War, op. cit.,* pp. 5, 38.

[11] *The Era of Atomic Power, op. cit.,* p. 53.

[12] *Christians and the Prevention of War in an Atomic Age* (London:
S.P.C.K., 1961), p. 42. The Commission met in 1956, 1957, 1958, 1960
and 1961.

of a "just war" does not really fit the situation as it now is, compared with the time when it was worked out in the late Middle Ages and the Renaissance.[13] As a result of this, the problem gets terribly bogged down in subtle discussions about who are innocents, what may be destroyed, who are responsible, what kind of weapons may or may not be used, and what kind of targets are legitimate, so that the whole argument becomes rather an exercise in casuistry than a genuine theological investigation. This is offset by the gentle and much more theological treatment of the question by what are called the Historic Peace Churches. These frankly refuse to be sidetracked toward the periphery and see in the conflict between war as such and the overriding primacy of love the heart of the matter. They have no difficulty in showing that Christ recognized no preferences of love based on biological or territorial boundaries, and they are the only ones who let the Gospel speak for itself in this matter. By the same token they cut short an ambiguity in the use of the word "love" which is obvious in the accusation leveled at them by Angus and Dun that they "distort love".[14] In the same way they deny that the pacifist is "socially irresponsible".[15] The record of the Quakers in the field of constructive social responsibility puts many other Christians to shame.[16]

There is no denying that all these documents show a deeply rooted but apparently invincible anxiety about the question whether there are two moralities, one Christian and one "natural", or only one. As early as 1932, Reinhold Niebuhr, whose name appears in almost every study, wrote: "Whenever religious

[13] *The Church and the Atom,* pp. 55-74.

[14] *The Christian and War,* pp. 7, 36-40.

[15] *Ibid.,* pp. 26-8, 40-4.

[16] Here is perhaps the place to mention some studies in this field of alternatives to war: Pyarelal, *Gandhian Techniques in the Modern World* (Ahmedabad, 1953); *The Economic and Social Consequences of Disarmament* (New York: U.N., 1962); T. Dunn (ed.), *Alternatives to War and Violence* (a symposium of 24 studies by experts in every field) (London, 1963); *Toward Peace and Equity* (New York: American Jewish Committee, 1946); *To the Counselors of Peace* (New York: American Jewish Committee, 1945); J. Bernal, *World without War* (London, 1958); and, finally, an interesting statement of the English hierarchy, *A Just and Lasting Peace* (London: C.T.S., 1945).

idealism brings forth its purest fruits and places the strongest check upon selfish desire it results in policies which, from the political perspective, are quite impossible. . . . It would therefore seem better to accept a frank dualism in morals than to attempt a harmony between the two methods which threatens the effectiveness of both. Such a dualism would . . . make a distinction between the moral judgments applied to the self and to others . . . and between what we expect of individuals and of groups." [17] The implication is plain that Christianity is irrelevant when applied to "others" or to "groups". Many non-pacifists have resented this cynical frankness but are not willing to admit that this statement only differs from the "just war" theory in the bluntness of its terms. That is probably why, in some subtle fashion, so many honest thinkers manage to accept and reject this theory at the same time. It "looks" different if we substitute "statesmen", "governments" or "rightful authority" or "the State" for Niebuhr's "groups", but that is only possible by implying that one's own responsibility is not involved in that of "governments" or the "State", and this would be hotly denied by the democratic Anglo-Saxon. And so, Stanley Windass has no difficulty in disposing of the theory. On the other hand, Paul Ramsey begins by showing that the modern presentation of the theory cannot be blamed on St. Augustine and then proceeds to make it the main pivot of a prolonged and tortuous argument in which all relevance gets lost in highly scholastic "special pleading".[18] It is not astonishing that, at the end of his peculiar manipulation of the "just war" theory, he extends the justice of a defensive war to a war "in order to effect our national purpose".[19] Apparently what is "national" is "just".

[17] *Moral Man and Immoral Society* (London: S.C.M., 1963), pp. 270-1.
[18] G. Windass, *op. cit.*, pp. 73ff.; P. Ramsey, *War and the Christian Conscience* (Durham, 1961); *idem*, "The Just War on Trial," in *Cross Currents* XIII/4 (1963), pp. 477-90; *idem, The Limits of Nuclear War* (New York, 1963); *idem*, "More Advice to Vatican II," in *Peace, the Churches and the Bomb* (New York, 1965). In this last essay Ramsey shows himself incapable of "listening", and spoils the discussion by misinterpreting his co-authors, Justus Lawler and Walter Stein.
[19] *War and the Christian Conscience*, p. 324.

Within the rather blurred boundaries of a rather mistrusted "just war" theory, many humanists and Christians found an outlet for their deeper anxieties in the discussion of the nuclear war as such, partly because of the wholly new dimensions this gave to the issue and partly because of the terrifying actuality of the nuclear arms race between the U.S.A. and the U.S.S.R., an actuality which is sharpened by the spread of nuclear weapons to other countries as well. The most important statement in this field came in the symposium on *Nuclear Weapons and Christian Conscience*.[20] It does not set out a particular thesis, except that Walter Stein frankly stands for what is called "nuclear pacifism", *i.e.*, a pacifism limited to the rejection of nuclear warfare. One cannot really say that the argument has been carried further in this book, although various points of current discussion are made with great sincerity and some pungency. The book was widely and favorably received in the press. Some progress has been made by Justus G. Lawler in his recent book *Nuclear War. The Ethic, the Rhetoric, the Reality*.[21] The author goes beyond most of his predecessors in stressing that, while much ink is flowing in arguing for or against the nuclear war, the positive side of the argument, brought out forcefully by *Pacem in terris,* is practically ignored, not least of all by the theologians. All these books refer to relevant literature in their own field, but there is no point in detailing it here because, as has been said, space is severely restricted.

In all this discussion there is strong reluctance to deal with the vast and ultimately decisive issues which Christianity must tackle. The discussion should bear on the nature of the Nation-State. It should examine whether a contingent political matter can demand of human persons, let alone fellow-members of

---

[20] W. Stein (ed.) (London, 1961). It contains essays by W. Stein, *The Defense of the West*, pp. 17-41, and *Prudence, Conscience and Faith*, pp. 125-51; the others are by G. Anscombe, *War and Murder*, pp. 45-62; R. Markus, *Conscience and Deterrence*, pp. 65-88; P. Geach, *Conscience in Commission*, pp. 91-101; and R. Smith, *The Witness of the Church*, pp. 105-22.
[21] Westminster, 1965.

Christ, to kill each other *without personal reasons*. It should ask whether the God-given dignity of the human person can be reduced to a political and material tool, whether as soldier or as victim. It should ask which human body can rightly claim to be invested with the authority to institute a process of war instead of a process of law. No person can take the law in his own hands, whether in Church or State. It should ask: "Who is my brother?" This question shows up a fantastic gap in present-day moral theology which is wholly conceived in terms of the individualistic mentality that has dominated the West for 600 years. It should examine the question whether we have not lost sight of the overwhelming implications of that "unity of mankind" of which recent popes have spoken in vain. It should explore the moral principles derived from this concept of mankind, in order that a new moral basis may be found on which to erect a sound system of international law with an international body of government and an international police force. It should examine not only the concept of authority but also that of love, which is wholly absent from the discussion. There are, of course, the jokers who immediately proclaim the family and the nation as having the first claim on our love. Unfortunately, Christ quite bluntly rejected such a physical and territorial limitation, which would reduce love to a mere extension of self-interest. It should examine the question whether the Christian can at a given point of distress throw Christianity overboard and follow an uncertain, ill-understood, man-made and man-adjusted "natural law" based on all kinds of half-redeemed, half-civilized instincts.[22] And this means nothing less than the ultimate issue of whether Christ is relevant or not. It is as simple as that, and as frightening as that, from the point of view of our very faith. It should examine basically whether the incarnate Christ implied a world order to be redeemed, protected and unified by violence or by constructive

[22] As J. Courtney Murray said: "The whole Catholic doctrine of war is hardly more than a *Grenzmoral,* an effort to establish on a minimal basis of reason a form of human activity, the making of war, that remains always fundamentally irrational" ("Remarks on the Moral Problem of War," in *Theological Studies* [March, 1959], p. 52).

witness and, if need be, suffering. There is not one genuine pacifist who washes his hands of the concrete misery of fear and violence. On the contrary, thus far only the genuine pacifist has actually done something about it.

It is, then, not astonishing that, when it comes to "theology", the pacifist puts up a far stronger case than the non-pacifist. The non-pacifist stands in agony before an insurmountable wall; the pacifist at least tries to undermine, climb over or get around it. Perhaps the first truly significant statement came in 1936, when Prof. G. H. C. MacGregor published his *New Testament Basis of Pacifism*,[23] a scrupulously fair and painstaking analysis of the Christian ethic based on the New Testament text. He points to the rise of a new group of non-pacifist Christians at the Amsterdam Conference of the World Council of Churches, who agree with Cardinal Ottaviani that "modern warfare, with its mass destruction, can never be an act of justice".[24] The general treatment, however, is still too much in the polemic style of somewhat antiquated apologetics.

The great theologian of pacifism, however, is Canon C. E. Raven who treated of the theological basis of pacifism in a great essay, *The Religious Basis of Pacifism*,[25] the main strands of which he developed afresh in his *Theological Basis of Christian Pacifism*.[26] I can only briefly summarize his argument here. Basically it is founded on the struggle between good and evil. After a sharp attack on Niebuhr, Schweitzer, Barth and Brunner whom he accuses of proposing Christianity as an irreconcilable conflict between Graeco-Roman "illumination" and biblical "redemption", he suggests that a Christianity that accepts a totally

---

[23] New edition (Glasgow, 1952).

[24] *Op. cit.,* p. 96.

[25] In a volume of essays entitled *The Universal Church and the World of Nations,* published as a follow-up to the Oxford Conference of 1937 (London, 1938). It is incredible that subsequent authors have so completely ignored this volume which contains more real argument on more real issues than many volumes on so-called "nuclear pacifism" or in defense of the "just war". Canon Raven's essay is the last (pp. 287-315).

[26] The lectures were given in 1950; the book did not appear until 1952 in London (Fellowship of Reconciliation).

evil nature and a world of grace as a Kierkegaardian "either-or" situation is an Arian Christianity which represents the creator and the redeemer as radically disparate. The whole meaning of Christ is that of victory over evil through the cross and resurrection. In other words, for him the non-pacifist position which accepts two orders, one of "justice" and one of "love", one of the Old Testament and one of the New Testament, one of the God of power and one of the God of love, is wholly irreconcilable with genuine Christian theology. And in this *tension,* which certainly exists but is contained within the unity of the incarnation, the problem of war is crucial because it represents the whole gamut of values of our relationships with God and our fellowman. He rejects, therefore, any appeal to a natural law against the law of love and maintains that as Christ came to fulfill the old law by the new, so the Christian cannot play up the natural law against the new but must transform the order of power and so-called natural justice by the order of love. This implies the suffering of the cross, which he accuses the Church of having failed to keep before the eyes of the faithful in order to find room for accommodation to the Manichaean concept of an evil and a good world. The basic struggle between good and evil lies within the human self, and as the Christian identifies himself with Christ, he has no choice but to seek victory in the way Christ achieved victory: through love and, if necessary, through suffering. The resources of his strength are then nothing but the application of faith, hope and charity, and the communion in the fellowship with others in the Spirit. "Christian pacifists derive their conviction not from the negative abhorrence of war nor from the utopian dream of a lotus-eater's world, but from the fact and significance of Jesus Christ." [27] One cannot therefore accept the suggestion of some theologians like the late Archbishop Temple and others who, at the beginning of World War II, suggested that in God's plan the establishment of justice and law must precede the reign of love: this would simply disrupt the continuity of salvation history by reintroducing a period of Old Testament

[27] *The Theological Basis of Christian Pacifism,* p. 19.

ethics periodically when the Christian ethic seems too demanding. Once again, if world and God are so wholly foreign to each
other that we can maintain an unredeemed natural justice whenever the redeeming love of the Father contradicts our instincts,
"then any true union of God and man in the one Christ becomes
impossible".[28] Thus the issue of war is an issue which radically
and communally is the test of whether Christianity is truly relevant or not. One cannot theologically get out of this basic di-
lemma by suggesting that pacifism is a kind of exceptional
charisma bound up with a special vocation or some peculiar
kind of evangelical counsel. It is a matter of the radical implications of love as the basic commandment and the very foundation
of the Christian ethic; a matter of the basic identification of the
Christian with Christ; a matter of whether Christ himself is genuinely significant for this world or not.

Even if this argument be conceded, there remain phenomenal
difficulties. The basic difficulty is that, while we might accept it as
applying to the individual Christian, we do not see how it applies
to human society at large. The problem is clearly perceived, not
only by pacifists,[29] but also by half-pacifists[30] and non-pacifists.[31]
All refer wistfully to "some effective international authority"
or some "world federation". But instead of taking this difficulty
by the horns and tackling it in depth, they let the argument too
easily slide off into accusations directed against the pacifist for
being unrealistic or unconcerned. But emotional accusations do
not constitute a theological argument.

The real point is that for the last six centuries the mentality
of the West has been so soaked in individualism that "person"
and "individual" have become identical in Western thought. The
result of this has been that the unity of mankind has become an
abstraction, a theory. Consequently, the most current concept
of "community" is that of small physical groupings such as the

---

[28] *Op. cit.*, p. 41.
[29] For example, *The Christian and War*, p. 6.
[30] For example, W. Stein and J. Lawler.
[31] For example, Dr. McReavy and P. Ramsey, and some of the Church
of England documents quoted above.

family or the clan, or territorial groupings such as the parish, the diocese and the nation. But these accidental and contingent groupings do not provide the concept of "community" with a solid ontological basis. Yet, the whole theology of creation and redemption presupposes the primacy of the human community as a whole. This is clearly recognized in Chapter II of the *Constitution on the Church*.[32] For this reason I have suggested that we should take the ontological oneness of human nature as the ontological foundation of the human community as a whole.[33] This is not new, but the consequences and implications of this have sadly failed to be taken seriously, and this seems to be the reason why this "unity of mankind", frequently referred to by recent popes, particularly Pope John, has not really penetrated into present-day theological and philosophical renewal. Yet, this would lift the whole "personalist" perspective out of a system of individualistic contortions and put it into line with the theological and concrete condition of man. This would inevitably lead to a new valuation of the "brother"; it would allow moral and dogmatic theologians to put morality on a much more realistic basis; it would provide a more fruitful basis for the ecumenical movement. The personal dignity of the "brother" would no longer be a mere adjunct to our individual existence, but he would be incorporated, and find his true place, in our concept of ourselves and of Christ. In this perspective the theological and practical implications of Christ's incarnation and redemption, of salvation history, would begin to make sense.

Now, from the practical point of view, one of the immediate consequences is that the whole question of nationalism and na-

[32] "It has not been God's resolve to sanctify and save men individually, with no regard for their mutual connection" (C.T.S. translation, p. 15).
[33] T. Westow, "Our Society: Open or Closed?" in *Front Line* 2 (1963), pp. 36-48; *idem*, "The Communion of Saints," in *Pax Romana Journal* (Christmas, 1963), pp. 3-6; *idem*, "Who Is My Brother?" in *Life of the Spirit* 18 (1964), pp. 466-78; *idem*, "Politics and Peace," in *Slant* 1 (1965), pp. 27-9; *idem*, "The Christian and the State," in *Reconciliation Quarterly* 129 (1965), pp. 542-7. As applied to the basis of ecumenism, cf. *idem*, "The Ecumenical Movement and the Laity," in *Search* III/10 (1965), pp. 370-6.

tional sovereignty, so rightly denounced by Pope Paul, would be reduced to its proper proportions. This danger of nationalism —which is taken for granted by all the authors who still more or less adhere to the "just war" theory—was already foreseen by the Marquess of Lothian in a powerful essay, *The Demonic Influence of National Sovereignty*.[34] It has led to the crippling and de-moralizing attitude of some members of the hierarchy during the war, as was made evident in the painfully fair and penetrating study of Prof. G. Zahn.[35] The same influences can be seen to damage the moral authority of the Church when nationalism is linked with an ideological conflict, as has been shown in the brilliant study by Prof. Leslie Dewart on *Cuba, Church and Crisis*.[36]

A historical examination of the problem of national sover-eignty as it is taken for granted in the "just war" theory shows that the Nation-State is a rather recent historical phenomenon, purely contingent in nature. This means that what is taken as representing an "absolute authority", such as might have the right to declare war, has no philosophical or theological founda-tion in fact. This point, adumbrated by Oscar Cullmann, I have tried to develop myself.[37] Basically, the right to make such ab-solute communal decisions is vested in *the human community as such,* and can only be exercised by an authority which rightly represents this whole community.[38] It cannot, therefore, be said that the Nation-State has a fundamental duty *as such* to defend itself, since the Nation-State is not an absolute entity and has no absolute rights. The reference to Paul (Rom. 13) simply says that secular authority is part of the "order" of God (the verb used is *tasso,* which means "to order", not to "constitute" as the *Bible de Jérusalem* translates: St. Paul does *not* say that secular

---

[34] *The Universal Church and the World of Nations*, pp. 3-23.
[35] *German Catholics and Hitler's Wars* (London, 1963). I must add that, though the material is German, the thesis is general.
[36] London (1964); New York (1963).
[37] O. Cullmann, *The State in the New Testament* (London, 1963); T. Westow, *The Christian and the State, loc. cit.*
[38] *Ibid.*

authority is divinely "instituted"). The two pivots, therefore, on which the personal conscience is hinged are the person and the human community as a whole.[39] This implies the basic right to conscientious objection, which was already admitted in England in the middle of World War I.

The understandable worry whether "pacifism" is practicable or not can only be tackled seriously *after* the *principle* has been honestly accepted. It is only then, as Canon Raven said, that the fruitfulness and inventiveness of the human community will find the practical solutions: in other words, as Bishop Wright said, when our wish for peace has become a *voluntas* instead of a *velleitas*.[40] Therefore, in spite of what the authors of *Peace, the Churches and the Bomb* have said, what is required of the Church is a frank declaration of *principle,* based on God's self-revelation in Christ as set out in the Scriptures, *not* another "practical" statement on disarmament which the Church is not equipped to make.

And this is where the argument about pacifism now stands. It would seem obvious that Canon Raven was right in saying that it is not a border problem, but a crucial one, involving the whole issue of the significance and relevance of the Church in the secular world. It is sad that neither modern existential theology nor recent existential philosophy has the courage to tackle this most existential of all problems. Yet, that is what the layman faces when reading his Sunday paper as soon as he comes out of the Sunday Mass.

[39] *Ibid.*
[40] Introductory essay to *Peace, the Churches and the Bomb.*

Coenraad van Ouwerkerk, C.SS.R./*Wittem, Holland*

Theological Discussion in Holland and France on Modern Warfare

In this short bibliographical survey I shall have to confine myself to some views and opinions that stand out against the background of attitudes and arguments about modern war which are now more or less known everywhere. I shall therefore concentrate on new insights rather than give a complete survey.

The Debate in Holland

Some acquaintance with the Dutch literature on the problem establishes the fact that the problem of peace and war had been discussed more widely and more explicitly in reformed circles than among Catholics. I do not know of an important Catholic monograph on this subject, but on the Protestant side there appeared several relevant studies.

"De-theologization." An exception was the report of the general assembly of the *Thijmgenootschap* (a learned society in honor of J. A. Alberdingk Thijm, a layman who exercised a decisive influence on the restoration of the hierarchy in Holland in the 1850's) *De strategie van de vrede* (The Strategy of Peace),[1] in which this subject is approached from various scien-

[1] "Strategie van de vrede," in *Annalen van het Thijmgenootschap* 53 (1965).

tific angles.[2] It contains a remarkable contribution by J. Arntz, *De betekenis van de theologie voor de strategie van de vrede* (The Significance of Theology for the Strategy of Peace), in which he refers to what seem to be important insights which he had set out in a previous article, *Bijbel, vrede en oorlog* (Bible, Peace and War).[3] Arntz asks that we should "de-theologize" the problem of war. As an existential phenomenon, war of course has religious implications for a believer, but in its ethical norms and practical aspect war is a human problem that can only be solved by man and, starting from man, within the world. Even if one appeals to the love of the Gospel, we ought to realize that in such a question as war it is a matter of explanation, a human interpretation of the commandment of love. Here one should remember that love implies the ideal of discarding war, but that this ideal presupposes a situation and favorable circumstances in which this ideal can be realized. It would be a wrong way of arguing theologically if unqualified pacifism were to be considered the one and only immediate consequence of love. Arntz also wishes to strip the theory of the just war of its theological pretensions. Historically speaking, this theory was originally nothing but an attempt to contain a war which in principle was hardly justifiable. Detached from its proper limited purpose, this theory is often put forward as a Catholic position by which the right to make war is credited to the State as an essential and inalienable right. Instead of a relative limitation of war, it becomes an affirmation.

The Impossibility of Absolute Norms

In general, one may say that Dutch Catholics, certainly until recent times, are inclined to a *via media:* an actual atomic war must be rejected on principle; insofar as atomic weapons are concerned, general rejection is hardly tenable. On this point a

[2] Thus, for instance, F. Duynstee, *Het jus ad bellum in onze tijd;* H. Kempen, *Psychologie en de problemen van oorlog en vrede;* J. Thurlings, *De strategie can de vrede, sociologisch beschouwd.*

[3] J. Arntz, "Bijbel, vrede en oorlog," in *Wijsgerig perspectief op maatschappij en wetenschap* 4 (1964), pp. 16-29, esp. pp. 27-9.

pragmatic attitude is advisable. This is not merely a matter of sober realism but a responsible position, as is very clear from two authoritative publications on social ethics in recent years.[4] The statement that there is a tension between politics and ethics which makes it impossible to look for an extreme and therefore *simpliste* solution seems therefore important to me. Both absolute defenselessness and unconditional violence must be rejected because both attitudes deny the polarity between ethics and politics. A radical pacifism sacrifices political reality to ethical witness, while the other extreme, unconditional violence, puts power above ethics and the human dialogue.[5] Closely connected with this tension between ethics and politics is the constantly growing awareness that there are no purely theoretical and ethical norms for war, but that every norm for this complex phenomenon depends on the effective efforts put into the building of a new order of international law and on how much faith one has in these efforts. In *Vraagstukken der hedendaagse samenleving* (Problems of Contemporary Society) the question is even proposed whether the problem of war can be solved juridically or morally without further ado. As long as one sees in violence the only possibility of maintaining law in practice, the problem remains insolvable from the practical and ethical point of view. "The only solution is to outlaw war totally and yet to guarantee what is right. The first can be done by total disarmament, the second by a generally accepted administration of justice. One may call this an illusion, but when one has to accept war with its spiral escalation downwards and its extension, there is no middle course." [6] For the time being the *via media* seems to be a pragmatic position which can only be justified in the perspective of a strategy for peace. However, the political reality of today imposes a temporizing which can temporarily justify arma-

[4] J. Ponsioen, G. Veldkamp, *Vraagstukken der hedendaagse sameleving* (Bussum, 1956); *Welvaart, welzijn en geluk. Een katholiek uitzicht op de nederlandse samenleving* V (Hilversum-Antwerpen, 1963).

[5] Cf. *Ibid.*, pp. 35-47.

[6] Ponsioen and Veldkamp, *op. cit.*, pp. 401-2. See also the whole chapter, "Oorlog en Vrede," pp. 394-412.

ment. Here the middle course is therefore ethically justified not
so much as a principle but rather as a way which abandons the
"just war" more and more.[7]

The Protestant Debate

The debate on modern war is unthinkable in Holland without
the Protestant contribution which is the most important, both
in quantity and quality. The Protestant discussion centers curi-
ously on official statements by the Churches and encyclical
documents. I am passing over the statements of the provincial
and general Synod of the Reformed Church because in 1957/8
they reflected the traditional attitude.[8] During the twelve years
from 1952 to 1964 we notice a fascinating development in the
writings that have come out of the Reformed Church.

While in 1952[9] there was a simple plea for an ethical approach to the just war in general, it was only in 1962[10] that
atomic war began to occupy a central position as a problem of
its own. This led to a radical rejection of any use of atomic
weapons. Limited war with conventional weapons was not
covered by this rejection and it is not altogether clear how far
tactical atomic weapons are condemned unconditionally. Although this rejection of the use of atomic weapons is not considered an exclusively Christian judgment, the Synod is nevertheless of the opinion that the Gospel shows here at least a
minimum requirement of anyone who takes the peace and love

[7] The same opinion is set forth in J. De Valk, *Hedendaags denken over
bewapening, oorlog en vrede* (DO-C publ., n. 164), pp. 8ff.
[8] *Het oorlogsvraagstuk. Toelichting op de uitspraken van de generale
synode van de Gereformeerde Kerken van Assen 1957/8, en van de
Gereformeerde Oecumenische Synod van Potchefstroom 1958* (Kampen,
1965).
[9] *Herderlijk Schrijven betreffende het vraagstuk van oorlog en vrede,*
on behalf of the General Synod of the Dutch Reformed Church, at The
Hague, July 3, 1952; printed as Supplement III in *Het vraagstuk van de
kernwapenen* (The Hague, 1963), pp. 85-93.
[10] *Het vraagstuk van de kernwapenen.* A necessary addition to the
Herderlijk Schrijven of July 3, 1952, concerning the problem of war and
peace, it was accepted by the General Synod of the Dutch Reformed
Church at its assembly of July 26, 1962 (The Hague, 1963). Cf. esp. pp.
16-26 and 43-50.

of the Gospel seriously. According to the Synod this rejection in principle does not imply an unconditional condemnation of atomic weapons. It considers that the problem of atomic weapons is in fact so complicated, precisely because of its intricate links with the concrete political reality, that here a plea for immediate, unilateral and total disarmament would not touch the reality of the situation.

This document of 1962 provoked a fierce discussion[11] which concentrated above all on the question of how much authority should be attached to these statements. Some thought that the Church interfered here irresponsibly with the decisions of the political authorities and contained an encouragement of radical pacifism and conscientious objection on principle.[12] This debate forced the Synod to produce a further statement.[13]

[11] Before *Het vraagstuk der Kernwapenen* appeared in 1962, the discussion had already been in full swing in the periodical *Wending,* a monthly devoted to Gospel and culture. Between January, 1953, and the autumn of 1958, it published a series of important articles which undoubtedly influenced the *Herderlijk Schrijven,* mentioned above, and of which the principal ones are: A. van Leeuwen, "Oorlog als ultima ratio," in *Wending* 7 (1953), pp. 619ff.; L. Patijn, "Het probleem der atoomwapens," in *Wending* 13 (1958), pp. 71ff.; C. Dippel, "Atoombewapening: Collectivistische vlucht uit de geschiedenis," in *Wending* 13 (1958), pp. 280ff. The *Herderlijk Schrijven* prompted more fierce reactions in the press than in the periodicals. Cf., among others, A. van Leeuwen, "De dans om de gouden egel," in *Wending* 17 (1962), pp. 658ff. Two objections stand out: the *Herderlijk Schrijven* bypasses competent politicians and the military and addresses itself to the authorities and the people at large as a whole; it also presents its witness with an ethical and religious finality that leaves no room for further thought and discussion. With what authority and right can the Church do this?

[12] This was the protest made by Calmeyer, the Secretary of State for Defense, who spoke of "an exhortation to massive conscientious objection".

[13] *Woord en wederwoord.* A continuation of the discussion about the problem of atomic weapons, it was accepted by the General Synod of the Dutch Reformed Church in its assembly of June 30, 1964 (The Hague, 1964). A good commentary on this document was provided by T. Knecht, "Woord en Wederwoord in de schaduw van de bom," in *Wending* 20 (1965), pp. 144-65. The pacifist movement within the Reformed Church reacted in a negative manner in a pamphlet by Kr. Strijd and J. de Graaf, *Wederwoord op wederwoord,* which was a continuation of the discussion on the problem of atomic weapons (Lochem, 1965).

In the Reformed Church, more than in Catholic circles, radical pacifism is represented explicitly on the basis of the Gospel:[14] "The essence of this means [of total annihilation] has no relation whatever with salvation and redemption as given to us by Christ." [15] However, it is interesting that in Holland this form of religious pacifism is still marked by a certain realism; disarmament is proposed as a way and an appeal, not as an unrealistic decision for the present. Nevertheless, the Church is expected to make a radical prophetic appeal for ultimate disarmament, and she is reproached for a weakening in her prophetic message by concerning herself with partial issues of a tactical, political and military nature.[16]

The Debate in France

It is impossible for an outsider to report on the more subtle nuances of the discussion elsewhere, and so I have to restrict myself to a general survey dealing only with major publications.

Previous Assumptions. In an earlier phase of the discussion there were two symposia: one was *L'atome pour ou contre l'homme* (The Atom for or against Man);[17] the other appeared in a special number of *Lumière et Vie: Le chrétien et la guerre* (The Christian and War).[18] The first collection provides an excellent survey of the technical and historical situation, but

---

[14] This pacifist tendency led to the formation of the *Beweging Kerk en Vrede* (Movement of Church and Peace), which contains Christians from various Churches and religious groups. It includes Catholics, and I should add that there are ecumenical groupings in Holland, such as the *Pleingroep* and the *Sjaloom-groep,* which, though ecumenical in intention, are strongly Catholic and show pacifist tendencies. Apart from the pamphlet *Wederwoord op wederwoord,* already mentioned, mention must be made also of a recent report, *Geweldloze weerbaarheid* (Non-violent Defense) (Amsterdam, 1964).

[15] Kr. Strijd and J. de Graaf, *op. cit.*

[16] Cf. *ibid., passim.*

[17] *L'atome pour ou contre l'homme* (Paris, 1958). This collection contains excellent technical and historical documentation up till 1958.

[18] "Le chrétien et la guerre," in *Lumière et Vie* 7 (1958), n. 38, pp. 1-129. Mention must also be made of the important though older collection, *Guerre et Paix,* of the 40th *Semaine Sociale de France* (Lyons, 1953).

it proceeds on traditional lines in the contribution on morality;[19] an extremely detailed casuistic treatment concludes this contribution. In the second collection there is above all a striking essay by M.-D. Chenu, who shows by referring to historical instances (Augustine, medieval Christendom and Vittoria) that evangelical inspiration does not excuse theology from working out a doctrine on peace and war within this world. This theology will always consist of a confrontation between the Gospel and the developing situation of the human community. A theological view of war and peace depends on the phases and changes of a developing organization of the nations. Chenu reproaches the theology of the 17th and 18th centuries (from which we inherited the current teaching on the just war) with the inability to confront the Gospel with the political and social situation of that moment, so that it gave rise to an abstract theory inclining either to an evangelical puritanism or a purely political realism. The urgency of a development in theological reflection on war and peace is put forth powerfully by D. Dubarle.[20] The unification of the human community throughout the world and the growing social and cultural interdependence do not allow us any longer to appeal to the classical foundation of the theory of the just war, such as the independence and self-sufficiency of the Nation-State and the rights based on these factors. Insofar as atomic weapons are concerned Dubarle declines to take up a definite position because he thinks this to be a matter of prudent estimation and therefore the concern of a politician who is also a committed Christian rather than that of a theologian.

One is struck by the importance given in the French debate to theological thought on the problem of non-violence. Two Dominicans, Régamy and Jolif,[21] have particularly demanded

[19] A. de Soras, "Réflexion théologique," in *Atome pour ou contre l'homme*, pp. 107-67.
[20] D. Dubarle, "L'avenir de la doctrine philosophique et théologique relative à la paix internationale," in *Nouv. Rev. Théol.* 97 (1965), pp. 337-55 (first published in the collection *Kerk, oorlog en vrede* [Roermond-Maaseik, 1965]).
[21] P. Régamey, *Non-violence et conscience chrétienne* (Paris, 1958); P. Régamey and J. Jolif, *Face à la violence* (Paris, 1963).

that Catholics pay more attention to this neglected issue. Their studies clearly show that rejection of defense on the basis of the Gospel is not so much a theory leading inevitably, for instance, to a theoretical rejection of all war or atomic weapons in all circumstances, but rather an attitude and strategy which tries every time to overcome the threat of war and theoretical reflection about this threat by effectively trying to build up peaceful relations among people. The pragmatic position of this form of defense-rejection is clear from the fact that it does not lead to a logical consequence of anti-militarism and conscientious objection.

Attempts at a Synthesis

Without wishing to underrate the various pastoral writings of the French hierarchy[22] who have exercised a powerful influence on theological opinion, I am most impressed by two studies of a synthetic nature which are related to the problem of war: that of Joseph Comblin, *Théologie de la Paix*,[23] and that of René Coste, *Morale internationale*.[24]

Since readers of CONCILIUM already know the position of Coste,[25] I limit myself to some interesting observations of Comblin. His thought is characterized by two contradictory statements. On the one hand, he states that war is in itself an evil to which one can never consent freely and deliberately because it belongs to the order of violence; on the other hand, he ac-

[22] For these documents see *Documentation Catholique* which gives a regular chronicle.

[23] *Théologie de la Paix*, I, *Les principes* (Paris, 1960); II, *Les applications* (Paris, 1963).

[24] *Morale internationale. L'humanité et la recherche de son âme* (Bibl. de Théol., Paris-Tournai, 1964). In this connection the same author published some important studies, among them *Mars ou Jésus. La Conscience chrétienne juge de la guerre* (Lyons, 1962), and *Le problème du droit de la guerre dans la pensée de Pie XII* (sér. Théol. 51) (Paris, 1962).

[25] R. Coste, "Pacifism and Legitimate Defense," in *Concilium* 5 (Glen Rock, N.J.: Paulist Press, 1965), pp. 80-94. Coste represents the middle way.

cepts a duty and right to war because violence would not mean an absolute evil. In circumstances where all peaceful means have failed, one sometimes can and must seize on war as the last inevitable means of restoring peace and order. Inevitability, necessity and a justified aim play an important part in his judgment. However, his richly documented and carefully shaded argument lacks a theological analysis of this inevitability and this use of war and violence as a means. He accepts war as a compromise without, in my opinion, diagnosing or justifying this compromise as a theological problem.

With regard to the atomic war, Comblin, like Coste, tries a middle course. He does not radically reject a tactical atomic war, and he believes that he can justify tactical atomic weapons as a consequence. However, these positions should not be detached from the whole in which they are set. According to Comblin, the theory of the just war is but the negative aspect of a theology of peace which aims at a concrete program of action, independent of concrete political power and political conflict.

Here I have to conclude this rather too summary survey of the debate, but I would like to end by pointing out that, in my opinion, in both France and Holland the debate is at the moment going to concentrate on the last question, which is still far from clear, namely, how we can deal with a political reality which evidently forces us occasionally to act in a way which so flagrantly contradicts both the Gospel and humanity. There are indications in the relevant literature which reflects, perhaps only slightly, the growing general opinion that the *via media,* between absolute rejection of defense and unconditional violence, for which most people seem to opt, is not satisfactory and makes people ill at ease. While scientists have cast doubt on the political necessity of war, theologians and ordinary faithful are uncertain about what place this political necessity has in the religious and ethical argument about war. At this *impasse* in the discussion it seems to me that people turn more and more away from the theories about war and try to develop a practical attitude and a program for the construction of peace.[26] The theoretical discussion seems to have reached a stage where it makes itself superfluous.

[26] This tendency came to the fore in various interventions at the Council when this section of schema XIII was debated; see particularly the intervention by Cardinal B. Alfrink. Cf. F. Alting von Geusau, *De Kerk, internationale samenwerking en organisatie van de vrede* (DO-C publ., n. 219).

Franz Böckle/*Bonn, W. Germany*

Peace and Modern Warfare: Theological Discussion in Germany

This article* is not an attempt to present even a brief summary of the various utterances of theologians and Christian statesmen on the problem of peace and modern warfare. Those who require a recent synopsis in this matter may refer to the extensively documented study of Karl Hörmann, *Friede und moderner Krieg im Urteil der Kirche.*[1] Hörmann's work only confirms the general impression that one gets when inquiring after the position of Catholic theologians. Our moral theologians treat the problem of modern warfare largely within the traditional framework of the teaching on justifiable war. For this reason, their opinions appear consistent, unimaginative and rather unrealistic: war is an evil; thus, the peace effort is a serious obligation. An aggressive war is immoral; a defensive war, on the other hand, must be permitted as a last resort to safeguard a greater good. Atomic weapons are to be judged according to their controllability.

In his allocution to the Eighth International Medical Congress in Rome on September 3, 1954, Pius XII had this to say about the question: "Is modern 'all-out warfare', especially A.B.C. (atomic-bacteriological-chemical) warfare, permissible as a matter of principle? There can be no doubt, particularly in view of the untold horror and suffering induced by modern warfare,

---

* Written before publication of the *Pastoral Constitution on the Church in the Modern World.*
[1] Vienna, 1964.

that to launch such a war other than on just grounds (that is to say, without it being imposed upon one by an obvious, extremely serious, and otherwise unavoidable violation of justice) would be an 'offense' worthy of the most severe national and international sanctions. One cannot even in principle ask whether atomic, chemical and bacteriological warfare is lawful other than when it is deemed absolutely necessary as a means of self-defense under the conditions previously stipulated. Even then, however, every possible effort must be made to avert it through international agreements, or to place upon its use such distinct and rigid limitations as will guarantee that its effects will be confined to the strict demands of defense. Moreover, should the use of this method entail such an extension of the existing evil as would render man wholly incapable of controlling it, its use should be rejected as immoral. In such an instance it would no longer be a question of 'defense' against injustice, and of the necessary 'safeguarding' of legitimate possessions, but of the pure and simple annihilation of all human life within the radius of action. Under no circumstances is this to be permitted." [2]

For someone who had carefully studied the context of this statement, the discussion that followed—beginning, significantly enough, only after Pius' death—seemed all out of proportion. The question discussed was the meaning of "capable of control" and how Pius actually understood this phrase.

In December, 1958, Clemens Münster used this papal reference as the point of departure for an article in *Hochland*.[3] He asked: "Is the nuclear bomb able to be controlled?" and, applying the test of controllability to the effect of the weapon, tried to demonstrate that the weapon could not be controlled. Shortly after this, no less an authority than the long-standing advisor of Pius XII, Gustav Gundlach, S.J., in a lecture before the Catholic Academy in Bayern on February 2, 1959 in Würzburg, declared: "In any case, one cannot say that Pius XII made the use of nuclear weapons dependent upon the con-

[2] *A.A.S.* 46 (1954), p. 590 (*The Pope Speaks* 1 [1954] p. 349).
[3] *Hochland* 51 (1958), pp. 132ff.

trollability of their effects. The 'controllability' intended by the Pope does not refer directly to the effect of the weapons themselves, but to the human act of *using* them." [4]

Ernst Wolfgang Böckenförde and Robert Spämann rightly rejected this interpretation in an extensive "Reply to Fr. Gundlach". They call it a misinterpretation liable to be made only by one "who thinks that the existence of things created by man is a matter of pure (scientific) factuality without innate purposiveness, and thus that these things in themselves possess no qualities but receive them only by way of external attribution".[5] In their reply, the authors lean heavily on the argument that the "nature" of a thing created by man can be so directed toward evil that its use *in accord with its intrinsic purpose* is possible only in an immoral act (as, for example, a genuinely pornographic book). "In like manner, the human spirit can also invent weapons designed and built for such a degree of destruction that their very nature, despite the intentions of one using them, requires them to destroy without distinguishing between combatants and noncombatants beyond any possibility of defense. These weapons are directed necessarily—by reason of the inner structure given to them by their human inventor—toward intrinsically inadmissible destructive effects and are, therefore, immoral in themselves." [6] One must therefore, as Eberhard Welt pointed out in 1954,[7] speak not only of a quantitative change but of a qualitative change in weapons.

The majority of Catholic authors will not admit this qualitative change in weapons. They want to make the question of the admissibility of using such weapons depend solely upon the questions of the legitimacy of defense and of the purity of

[4] So, in any case, in the extended version published later both in "Kann der atomaren Verteidigungskrieg ein gerechter Krieg sein?" in *Studien und Berichte der kath. Akademie in Bayern,* Heft 10 (Munich, 1960), pp. 113f., as well as in *Stimmen der Zeit* 164 (1958/59), pp. 4f.

[5] "Die Zerstörung der naturrechtlichen Kriegslehre," in *Atomare Kampfmittel und christliche Ethik* (Munich, 1960), p. 193.

[6] *Ibid.,* p. 194.

[7] "Achtung des Atomkrieges," in *Die neue Ordnung* 8 (1954), pp. 129ff.

intention.[8] The unsatisfactory conciliar debate on this question as occasioned by "Schema 13", however, has shown that the distinction between aggressive and defensive wars is not adequate to answer the frightening moral questions of an atomic age. In certain circumstances, would not a defense with nuclear weapons in a "just" war be even more reprehensible than a limited "unjust" act of aggression with conventional weapons?

In any case, moral theology, with its categories of just defense and its norm of choosing the lesser evil, has not demonstrated the possibility of justifying an atomic war. But even if a clear consensus should decide that nuclear war is never allowed, still, the whole complex question of the race for nuclear armaments would not thereby find an "automatic" solution. The alternative of wholly condemning nuclear war or allowing it conditionally is falsely stated. Before going into this question (3), it is necessary not only to discuss briefly the question of Christian pacifism (2), but to clarify the far more basic question of the extent of the competence of the Church in treating these questions at all (1).

1. *Limits of the Church*

The Church, i.e., in this matter the universal magisterium— under which we may in a certain sense place theology considered as an ecclesial science—is overtaxed on two sides. The "clerical triumphalists" view the Church as the wise and experienced teacher of mankind; she knows just about everything needed for the peace and welfare of all peoples. These "triumphalists" expect the Church to give concrete instructions that have only to be followed by all to assure the true peace and welfare of humanity. The same opinion is held by the "lay defeatists" who expect from the Church exactly what the "clerical triumphalists" think they can provide. These "defeatists" complain when the Church authorities do not answer their demands. It was against

[8] Cf. J. Hirschmann, "Kann atomare Verteidigung sittlich gerechtfertigt sein?" in *Stimmen der Zeit* 162 (1957/58), pp. 284ff., esp. p. 290; O. Stockle, "Zum christlichen Gespräch über die atomare Bewaffnung," in *Orientierung* 23 (1959), pp. 30ff.

these excessive claims that Karl Rahner tried to delineate "the limits of the Church in regard to controlling innerworldly private and social situations".[9]

The unreasonable demands made upon the Church arise from a fundamental misunderstanding of her properly religious role. Rahner does not advise a return to the "religious ghetto". He knows well enough that Christ's incarnation and his redemptive passage through death into life have called man to a new relation with God and his fellowmen, and that this new relation deeply furthers human society. "But the decisive role of the Church regarding this [practical] Christianity in the world itself is not conveniently to set up concrete models of Christian behavior that man need only copy obediently, honestly and accurately to be a good Christian. The Church does not offer models for this life, but gives man the power to live life even without models . . . precisely through the fulfillment of the religious obligations most proper to it." [10]

This admonition is not original with Rahner; it has been passionately defended by prominent laymen whenever certain theologians—at least in some particulars of their opinions—have ventured too far into the area of political debate. The decisive dispute in Germany about our theme has always had a well-defined place, and the various opinions are interpreted falsely unless one recognizes the political background of the question. The concrete problem faced by the German parliament in the years since 1957 has been whether to equip the army with nuclear weapons. Both opponents and advocates have made it a matter of Christian conscience and both have appealed to the authority of Pius XII for support. In the process, a bitter argument arose concerning the competence of moral theology to deal with this issue, especially on the occasion of a "Word about Christian Peace, Politics and Nuclear Armament" [11] published

[9] K. Rahner, "Grenzen der Kirche," in *Wort und Wahrheit* 191 (1964), pp. 249ff.

[10] *Ibid.*, pp. 260f.

[11] *Herder Korrespondenz* 12 (1957/58), pp. 395ff.

by seven German Catholic moral theologians on May 5, 1958.
Although the authors were evidently careful to use well-balanced
formulas, they still believed that one was justified in saying:
"Even in a just war of defense, not every means of fighting
is permitted without question. If the means used completely
escape the control of man, such use must be condemned as
immoral. *That the effect of nuclear weapons completely escapes
control, must, in the judgment of conscientious experts, be considered an erroneous opinion. The use of such weapons, therefore, is not necessarily contrary to the moral order and is not
a sin in every case*." [12]

Peter Nellen, Walter Dirks and others could not understand
how the authors of this opinion (arrived at apparently in the
interests of party-politics) could possibly have considered that
the question of controllability—placed expressly by Pius XII
as a condition—had already been solved. Walter Dirks wrote in
an article with the illuminating title "The Dangers of Following
the Political Line":[13] "The shot in the dark by the authors
occurs in the first half of point 9. We find there a list of five
groups of 'differences of opinion' possible 'among Christians'.
. . . From this we should be able to conclude from a moral-
theological point of view that both ways of solving the problem
at issue are essentially open and both sides are protected from
defamation. Furthermore, we ought to conclude that the opposition between opinions (1) can be borne in a reasonable
manner, (2) can be lessened by more reliable information ap-
proaching more closely the actual facts of the case and by a
more careful examination of conscience orientated by valid
norms, and (3) may be resolved according to democratic rules
of play and morality, should the second possibility turn out to
be impracticable. Instead of this, the published declaration con-

---

[12] *Ibid.,* p. 396; cf. the preparatory study by J. Hirschmann, "Zur
Diskussion um die Wehrpflicht," in *Stimmen der Zeit* 159 (1956/57),
pp. 203ff., as well as the defense by the same author in note 8 *supra;* the
contrary position is held by P. Nellen, *Sieben Moraltheologen* (Nurem-
berg, 1958).

[13] *Frankfurter Hefte* 13 (1958), pp. 379ff.

fuses in many places statements of principles with assertions of fact. To this we may say that (1) theology is not competent to proceed in this manner, and (2) the seven moral theologians themselves have maintained in point 9 that their own estimate and evaluation remain in the area of possible Christian differences of opinion." [14]

We readily admit that we have to agree with the judgment of this "layman". Church and moral theology can do no more in fact than recall to mind the *principles* of right judgment; the *decision* itself—in particular, the political decision—must be left to the expert knowledge and conscience of the individual. Church and moral theology—prejudiced here in favor of a very questionable premise—have no right to insinuate that a specific practical conclusion has to follow necessarily even from principles that are correct in themselves.

2. The Kingdom of God and Temporal Power

The problem of keeping the message of Jesus free from extraneous elements and presenting it in its pure form has occupied Christianity from the very beginning. Fidelity to the Sermon on the Mount appeared not infrequently as the decisive criterion, and the sharp antithesis made by Jesus between all self-calculating morality and his radical demand for love appeared as the unconditional repudiation of any compromise with a manner of thought proper to the "world". One never lost sight, either, of the difficulties that naturally followed from this position for the Christian; the Christian, after all, lives in the world. Luther thought the solution lay in his doctrine of the two powers: the power of grace and love and the power of law that restrains sin. In the kingdom of grace are only kindness and forgiveness; in the kingdom of law, there must also be force, struggle and war. Man is subject to both powers.

Within the Catholic tradition, a solution of the tension was not sought in a dialectic, but in a synthesis of love and justice, of Christian freedom and civil freedom. Civil (political) and

[14] *Ibid.,* pp. 387f.

Christian freedom are not the same entity: the politically or socially enslaved believer is still a liberated Christian; the politically or socially free believer is still a slave of Christ. God can make use of political or social slavery to help us distinguish and recognize anew the incomparable value of Christian freedom, for this freedom can exist even in a situation of political slavery and, in such a situation, can first begin to show its true value. The boundaries of true freedom and slavery are not coextensive with political boundaries; even in the midst of the worst terrorism, a call toward, and a life in, Christian freedom is possible. For this reason, the laudable principle "rather death than life in slavery" is not, from a Christian point of view, the last word of wisdom.

From all we have just said, it is not surprising that it is easier to find *well-known* defenders of a more or less uncompromising pacifism among Evangelical theologians than among Catholic theologians, and that, from a purely quantitative point of view, their voices predominate in the literature on the question (which does not actually say much about the position of the faithful as a whole). It is often difficult to determine whether they agree with us or not because they are concerned directly and exclusively with the question of the legitimacy of modern war without bothering to define more clearly the legitimacy of war in se, whereas Catholic theologians seem to spend too much time on the latter question. In 1956, the assembly of the EKD (Evangelical Church in Germany) declared in its deliberations on the legal arrangements for protecting conscientious objectors: "If the whole issue of war has become more serious than ever before for Christians today, it is not because of the acceptance of a general principle of not using force, but because the Word of God is taken more earnestly. The differences among Christians regarding war derive from different explanations of the Word as law and Gospel, even within the Evangelical Churches. In view of the various positions taken by the Churches regarding the problem of participation by Christians in war, the

Evangelical Church of Germany, in accord with her previous standpoint contained in her synodal declarations, must allow the possibility of participation as well as refusal of participation, both of which can be justified from a Christian point of view." [15]

None of the later official or unofficial statements have gone beyond this conclusion, although they betray ever more clearly an increasing dissatisfaction with such a solution. The honesty with which this has been admitted could perhaps serve as an example for us. On April 16, 1958, the Lutheran bishops' conference declared, in reference to nuclear war: "Theological, political and moral declarations that do not go beyond non-obligatory generalizations are necessarily ineffective. Appeals to man's sense of anxiety only increase world panic. Proposals that oversimplify the situation and do not indicate a way toward practical implementation cannot satisfy the Christian conscience." [16] And in 1960, an interim report of the EKD assembly's commission on atomic questions stated conclusively: "The commission feels it necessary to warn against a too hasty acceptance of complementarity—a notion arising out of the attempt to overcome a contradiction—as the key to the problem. This notion must first be tested in practice for its serviceability in reconciling contrary ethical decisions." [17]

It is a fact that there is even a certain mutual relationship

[15] *Kirche und Kriegsdienstverweigerung* (Munich, 1956), pp. 13f.

[16] *Christusbekenntnis im Atomzeitalter?* ed. E. Wolf (Munich, 1959), p. 105.

[17] *Evangelische Welt* 14 (1960), pp. 116f. Besides these official positions, we indicate here a few individual statements which are particularly important, without—even less than in treating Catholic authors—trying to include everyone. The range of opinions runs from extreme left to extreme right. A. Schweitzer, *Friede oder Atomkrieg?* (Munich, 1958); M. Niemoller, *Reden 1958-1961* (Frankfurt, 1961); H. Gollwitzer, "Die Christen und die Atomwaffer," in *Theol. Existenz heute,* new series 61 (Munich, 1957); *Atomzeitalter, Kreig und Frieden,* ed. G. Howe (Witten, 1954); H. Thielicke, *Die Atomwaffe als Frage an die christliche Ethik,* (Tübingen, 1958); K. Barth, *Kirchliche Dogmatik* III, 4, pp. 515ff.; W. Kunneth, "Atomrüstung und Ethos," in *Zeitwende* 32 (1961), pp. 234ff.; E. Gross, *Das Geheimnis des Pazifismus* (Stuttgart, 1959).

between political and Christian freedom. The Christian consciousness has always insisted upon a practical equality of recognition and rights for all men. Even when Christians did not act directly as reformers of the existing social order, the Church's message still remained a catalyst for an irresistible revolutionary force that gradually renewed society. The visible expression of Christian freedom in the area of human relations is a mark of concrete Christian convictions. Civil-social freedom and Christian freedom must be neither identified nor completely disjoined; otherwise, two thousand years of Christianity would never have led to the abolition of social discrimination. The free world owes, even if unknowingly, its freedom to an authentically Christian understanding of freedom. The blessing of freedom, won in centuries-long struggle, has a right to existence and must not be surrendered thoughtlessly.

We must not begin a return to a supposedly "pure" world-disinterested Christianity that has never existed in reality. The current reduction of Christian freedom to a purely interior freedom of faith has always been a distortion that restricts its inner dynamism and power of radiation. For the sake of freedom itself and out of love for the Christian people, such a reduction should not now be accepted without opposition.

When force is used to avoid a real crime, it is not an evil, but love in disguise. This is why Catholic tradition has never looked upon the right to defense of individuals and society as foreign to Christian thought; that right is rather the actualization of this thought in the given reality of our existence, marked as it is by sin. Such a right to defense does not, however, enjoy absolute validity; it is limited by the purpose and by the means used. The purpose may not consist primarily in the destruction of opponents, nor in revenge, but only in the defense of corporal, and especially, spiritual and eternal existence. When, therefore, a nuclear war can mean the end of the earthly existence of humanity, it would be absurd to call the destruction of humanity a means of saving it. We do not see herein—contrary to Gundlach—any admissible manifestation of God's majesty. Defense has meaning only when there is something left worth defending.[18] As to the means of defense, it can at least be said that they may not be employed as instruments of mass destruction.

While there is now a surprising unanimity among Catholic theologians regarding these principles, a conclusion condemning wars of mass destruction is less unanimous. When an official conclusion is drawn (somewhat as at the Council) from fundamental considerations, the magisterium ought to restrict its pronouncements to statements of decisive principles and leave their application to statesmen, and hope they may be right. But the impression should not be conveyed that one really—hidden under forceful appeals for peace—wants to suggest conditional approval of nuclear war, thus leaving the door open for a further step-up in the armaments race. Between the false alternative of either a *general condemnation* or a *conditional approval* of *nuclear war,* the question of nuclear mobilization must be considered a separate problem.

The Question of Nuclear Mobilization

War and preparation for war, despite their intimate connection, must be kept separate. The question of mobilization presents those responsible with a clear alternative: *either* the West steps up its nuclear mobilization in the hope that this will reduce the threat from the other side so that the "balance of terror" will prevent an actual war, *or* one rejects on principle and unilaterally the production and use of nuclear weapons in the hope that this will clear the air so that one's own repudiation will morally obligate the opponent to also reject the use of those

[18] "Even in the possible case that there remains only a testimony to God's majesty and his design (which we owe him as human beings), the right and duty of defending ultimate values is still thinkable. Even should the world perish thereby, that would not be an argument against our position." G. Gundlach, *op. cit., supra* note 4, pp. 131 and 13. How far this sharpening of the question divides opinions is shown by A. Auer: "The natural law dictates that the use of the nuclear bomb is permitted under the conditions stipulated. There is only one definitive limitation on its use: the case of a nuclear explosion resulting in an uncontrollable chain reaction that would place all human life in danger." "Atombombe und Naturrecht," in *Die neue Ordnung* 12 (1958), p. 264.

weapons. Neither possibility is promising: the first is a game of self-destruction; the other envisions the utopian possibility of a high-principled democrat imposing his norm of action upon a mad dictator. Nevertheless, one must consider the fact that the terrible "balance of terror" offers at the moment a certain "non-aggression guarantee" ("peace guarantee" would be saying too much!). For a realistic statesman, this is surely something positive and definite here and now, whereas the possibility of a catastrophe does not have such immediate significance or certainty. The effective avoidability of that catastrophe cannot be excluded from the realm of real possibilities! The question whether and to what extent fighting with nuclear weapons will occur is, therefore, as an element of the future, a necessary object of careful prognosis.

One cannot proceed, therefore, to a so-called moral solution to the problem of using nuclear weapons and tag the alternatives with the labels "approved" or "rejected" so as to justify or condemn the whole question of nuclear armaments from this aspect alone. Such a general consideration and judgment is quite unsatisfactory. To ignore the distinction between mobilization with nuclear weapons and the actual use of these weapons shows, moreover, how remote one considers the real possibility of effectively avoiding actual conflict. But this is to encourage a disastrous fatalism! The extremely complex political, strategic and psychological problem of preparing for modern warfare cannot even begin to be solved merely by investigating the moral value of a determined weapon!

It is certain that serious preparation for nuclear war includes a readiness to use the potential acquired. In spite of this, readiness to use must be clearly distinguished from actual use, especially in circumstances subject to continual change. There is need for partial decisions, dependent upon many varying factors, and these decisions must be taken and justified by statesmen according to the situation of the moment. We do not think it right to say that a clear condemnation of all-out war would mean that mobilization itself is already wrong. This is too abstract a view of things. The concrete reality is that humanity finds itself in a blind alley. Everyone obviously realizes that a totally destructive war is no way out, surely not a legitimate way, and to seek a "solution" in this direction is evil. The solution, therefore, can lie only in progressive disarmament. It is of decisive importance that we believe unswervingly in this goal. This goal must inspire our every step, even the paradoxical decision to increase temporarily our military strength. Such a paradox is part of the blind-alley situation.

What can the Church do in this situation? She certainly cannot invent political formulas. It is not enough, either, for her simply to remind men of the first principles of moral judgment. The world and its statesmen are not helped to a decision by conditional approval or unconditional rejection of nuclear weapons. Walter Dirks was right in saying, in an unpublished memo: "If the Council does not have anything else to offer except a political 'approved' embellished with a nonpolitical moral appeal, then it will have failed in politics and lost its moral credit in the eyes of the world." One must finally rid oneself of a naive pride in a very limited morality for which there exist no objective "entanglements" or "blind alleys", and which can indicate for every situation at any moment a legitimate and an illegitimate, a correct and a false solution.

Dirks asks that the Church speak in terms of this "blind alley", that she admit her partial confusion and make clear that all of us are guilty of this tragic situation through our sins. "The situation in which the world finds itself is essentially the consequence of actions and guilt within Christianity!" From this point of view and with this attitude, a forceful appeal for recognition of a final effort to establish a just mutual control of armaments could have some chance of success.

PART III

DOCUMENTATION
CONCILIUM

Office of the Executive Secretary
Nijmegen, Netherlands

Arthur McCormack/*London, England*

The Church and the Population Explosion

The fourth session of Vatican Council II, with the exception of the speeches by Bishop Marling of Jefferson, U.S.A. and Archbishop Simons of Indore, India, made little reference to the population explosion. Neither did the *Constitution on the Church in the Modern World** have a great deal to say about it, although what it said was good.

On the other hand, sensational articles in books and periodicals threaten disaster for the human race unless a drastic population policy is imposed to reduce "the menace of numbers". Outside the Church the population expansion seems to be regarded as the number one problem; inside the Church it seems to have aroused little interest.

DIFFERENT VIEWS ON THE PROBLEM

Views on the subject of the population explosion vary, from those held by people—often Catholics—who see no cause for alarm and rely on the fact that the bounty of the world can feed its peoples, to the other extreme where it is boldly stated that economic goods are the only things in life that make for happi-

---

* This article was written before the publication of the Pastoral *Constitution on the Church in the Modern World.*

ness and that, if there are a great number of people to share these goods, then there will be less for each; hence the need for drastic population control achieved by *any* effective means regardless of morality and human dignity.

Mr. Colin Clark in England and Father A. Zimmerman[1] in Japan represent the first, over-optimistic view, although it would be unfair, especially to the latter, to suggest that they are uninfluenced by other views. The other, pessimistic view is held by some doctrinaire family planners, especially in the United States, who have allowed themselves to become so obsessed by population problems that they see almost all other economic and social problems in this light.

In between these extremes, there are many shades of opinion. On the whole it may be said that American demographers of the Princeton school, of the Population Council in New York and of the Population Reference Bureau in Washington (e.g., Professor Ansley Coale, Frank Notestein, Robert Cook) tend, in differing degrees, to stress the numerical increase in population in the world and the need for population policy above all else. Although they admit the need for economic measures to deal with the situation, nevertheless, population control still emerges in their writings as the most important factor, while other measures for combating world poverty—for example, the agricultural revolution—are played down. This might even be said of Richard M. Fagley[2] whose concern about the population problem and the lack of interest shown by the Churches sometimes makes him appear less moderate than he really is. At the darker end of the spectrum of opinions, Sir Julian Huxley, one of the pioneers of demography, tends to exaggerate its dimensions and effects out of all proportion. In a similar vein is *Our Crowded Planet*,[3] a symposium edited by Fairfield Osborn (whose book *Our*

[1] *Cf. Catholic Viewpoint on Overpopulation* (New York: Hanover House, 1961).

[2] *The Population Explosion and Christian Responsibility* (O.U.P., 1960).

[3] *Our Crowded Planet* (edited by Fairfield Osborn) (London: Allen & Unwin, 1963).

Plundered Planet, published three years after the end of World War II, was one of the first books to sound a warning about demographic increase, and which, although extreme, was valuable in parts).

Less extreme and of high scientific quality, with the complicated nature of the problem illustrated from widely differing fields such as economics and gynecological research—although it can be said that one or two of the papers are lacking in scientific objectivity—is *Human Fertility and Population Problems,*[4] the published proceedings of the seminar sponsored by the American Academy of Arts and Sciences, edited by Roy Greep.

A symposium, edited by Dean William E. Moran Jr.—the papers of the 37th Annual Conference of the Catholic Association for International Peace held in Washington, D.C., October 22-25, 1964—has gone a long way toward dispelling the reproach that Catholics have shirked consideration of the population explosion. This book, *Population Growth—Threat to Peace?,* has papers by such distinguished non-Catholic experts as Irene Taeuber and Oscar Harkavy of the Ford Foundation, as well as Catholics such as George Schuster, John L. Thomas, S.J., and George Dunne, S.J. It is a sober examination of the serious nature of population growth and its effects in various fields, and it is notable for its balanced and holistic approach. Perhaps the best commendation of it is that it does not reach any hard and fast conclusions or advocate any panaceas. "There is no single and simple solution to this extremely complex problem. The contributors to this volume are all aware of how complex the problem really is; this awareness, of course, should lead only to determination on our part to mobilize all our forces to attack the problem more vigorously."[5]

This attitude is also typical of the work of the French professor, A. Sauvy, perhaps the greatest population expert in the world. In *Fertility and Survival*[6] he is rather sceptical of popula-

[4] Cambridge, Massachusetts: Schenkmans Publishing Company, 1963.
[5] New York: P. Kenedy, 1965.
[6] London: Chatto & Windus, 1961.

tion policies and stresses economic advance in the short term as the best available approach.

The series of population conferences for the three years 1963, 1964, and 1965, held under the presidency of George Schuster of Notre Dame University in Indiana, have also made a very valuable contribution to the Catholic awareness of population problems. The first book of papers and discussions was especially valuable, dealing as it did with moral and theological considerations; Vol. II, *The Problem of Population,*[7] was more concerned with the American scene and "practical Catholic applications". Both volumes represented a good cross-section of Catholic thought in the crucial field of Catholic attitudes to means of population control. From the third of these meetings came the statement submitted to the papal commission on birth control, a document deserving of great consideration on account of the distinction of the contributors and the honesty of their thought. In some areas it was not unanimous but showed great concern for responsible parenthood in the face of the population explosion and family problems.

The work of Professor Cépède, Abbé Francois Houtart and Linus Grond, O.F.M., published as *Population and Food* [8] is also worthy of note for its extremely thorough and factual examination of the whole problem from the point of view of food resources relative to population growth, and also for its sociological observations. The authors regard some of the population policies proposed as alibis—not without reason—and say that "although much of the planet has been plundered by the men who inhabit it, and although other parts of it remain an undeveloped wasteland, still it yet provides them with the means for overcoming these limiting factors upon the multiplying of their species".[9]

[7] *The Problem of Population* I (edited by Donald Barrett); II (edited by George Schuster) (Indiana: Notre Dame Press, 1964).
[8] New York: Sheed & Ward, 1964.
[9] *Op. cit.,* p. 443.

The Work of the United Nations

On the whole one can say that Catholics who have made a thorough scientific study of population problems have made a worthwhile and balanced contribution. The same cannot be said of some of the superficial articles that have appeared, especially in America, where Catholic non-experts have allowed themselves to take over more extreme views of one side or the other. The sensational writing of William Vogt and S. Chandrasekhar in the New York Times, at the time of the meeting of the United Nations Population Commission in March and April of 1965, stressing the "menace of numbers", is also to be deprecated. Although these men are scientifically competent, they show the partisanship which has so often marred discussion of this poignant problem of population, and Vogt, although a soil expert, does not base his views on the latest work in his own field.

The United Nations Population Commission has done magnificent work—especially its Secretariat—in providing facts and figures on every aspect of the complicated problems of demography. Paper 186 [10] of January, 1965, for that year's session of the commission is one of the most comprehensive and balanced appraisals of population and development problems yet produced.

In a speech at the United Nations Population Commission on March 24th, Dr. B. R. Sen, Director General of F.A.O., although pressed strongly to come out with a clear endorsement of birth control policies, did not do so, but he did highlight the fact that, in many of the poorer parts of the world, population is increasing faster than agricultural productivity, which needs to be stepped up considerably if we are to avoid disastrous famine situations in the next ten or fifteen years.

A leading F.A.O. expert on soil, Dr. Luis Bramao, has recently stated boldly (in an interview in *The Long Island Catholic,* October, 1965, commenting on Pope Paul's speech at the United Nations) that the problem in some underdeveloped coun-

[10] DO.C E/CN 9/186 of the UNESCO.

tries is not overpopulation but underpopulation, explaining that Brazil's population of eighty million is equivalent to France having a population of only 500,000 people, "and where would France be today if she had so few?"

The Asian Population Conference at New Delhi, December 10-20, also took a very balanced view of the population situation in Asia. Population restriction policies came only seventh in order of priorities. The first Latin American Conference on Population held in Cali, Colombia, August 11-14, 1965, was also very balanced in its approach, but was concerned, naturally enough, with the obstacles that rapid population growth poses to economic advance in Latin America and advocated that each nation should adopt a population policy. It did not stress sufficiently the fact that South America is an empty continent. However, it did rightly say: "The realization of dangers deriving from demographic growth and the policies which may be adopted or applied on that subject should not distract attention from the necessity for basic economic and social reforms."

In a brief survey it is only possible to give an impressionistic view,[11] but I hope it serves to show the wide range of reactions to the problem of the population explosion. For the non-expert to be able to form an intelligent opinion amid so much confusion, the facts must be considered objectively, stripped of the interpretations and theories and solutions proposed by interested parties. Discussions of population problems, especially in the popular media of communications, often generate far more heat than light. What are the *facts?* What is the population situation in the world today and in the foreseeable future?

[11] I have not dealt, e.g., with the World Population Conference of Belgrade, 1965, which would need an article by itself; also, I have not referred to *The Population Crisis* (edited by Larry K. Ng of the University of Indiana Press, 1965), a very complete treatise in the form of a symposium on the subject from many aspects with interesting and useful documentation from United Nations sources, the proceedings of the French Social Week at Angers in 1959, and a valuable Italian symposium edited by Professor Vito (1962), *Il Problema Demografico.*

WHAT ARE THE FACTS?

It is as impossible to understand these without reference to statistics as it would be to discuss Scripture without reference to the actual texts. I must crave the reader's indulgence for producing these—most people find a welter of figures distasteful—and I will try to give them in the simplest possible form. All the figures I give are taken from United Nations documents, mainly those produced by the United Nations Population Commission and the latest United Nations Demographic Yearbook published in October of 1965.[12]

According to the latest United Nations projections of the future growth of world population which, in 1960, had just reached 3,000 million or three billion (it is now 3,265 million), we will have between 5,300 million and 6,800 million people by the end of this century. The figure expected, based on medium expectations as distinct from the low and high projections just quoted, is in the area of six billion.

These statistics enable us to see at a glance what the population explosion of this century has involved. The population of the world in 1900 was estimated at 1½ billion people; at mid-century it was 2½ billion. By the year 2000, it will be four times the amount it was at the beginning of the century. As we have seen, world population will have doubled between 1960 and the year 2000.

It took the human race from the beginning of its existence until the year 1650 to reach the 500 million mark; the population of the world increased by that amount in the twelve years between 1950 and 1962.

But these global figures do not give the full picture. The population explosion is all the more serious because it is taking place largely in the less developed continents of Latin America, Africa and Asia. In the developed countries of the West, Japan and Oceania, the increase of population is estimated at half a billion

---

[12] There are statistics for some countries available which are more up to date, but I ignore these for the sake of uniformity and comparison.

in all by the year 2000. In the less developed regions of the world the increase will be 2½ billion, i.e., from 2 billion in 1960 to 4½ billion at the end of the century. Recent trends suggest even higher figures.

In other words, for every 100 people in the developed countries in 1960, there will be 160 at the end of this century, while for every 100 people in the less developed countries in 1960, there will be approximately 300 by the year 2000.

To put it in a more striking and easily assimilated way, 35 years from now, 75% of the world's population will be in the countries now classified as underdeveloped. By the end of the century the population of Asia will be as large as the total population of the world today.

The figures I have given are, I stress, the sober projection of experts, based on actual and expected rates of population increase. Rates of population growth—or of natural increase, which is the term generally used—are calculated on the difference between crude birth rates and death rates (ignoring migration). Thus, if a country has an annual crude birth rate of 40 per thousand and a death rate of 20 per thousand, its rate of population growth or natural increase will be 20 per thousand of its present population, or, expressed as a percentage as it usually is, 2% per annum.

The present population of the world is approximately 3,265 million, and its rate of natural increase is 2%. Therefore, the population of the world is increasing at present by 65 million per year, more than the total population of Great Britain. Every day there are 170 thousand more mouths to feed; every minute there are 118 more units added to the human sum.

This survey of the population situation, however impressionistic, is adequate, I think, to show that we are facing an entirely unprecedented phenomenon. It is the increased rate of growth which is the main problem, and it is this that makes attempts to deal with the problems of population growth, either by economic and agricultural advance or population restriction policies, extremely difficult. It is very important to realize this and to understand that the lessons of the past in the developed countries are for this reason inadequate guides in the entirely new circumstances of today.

Is the world then already overpopulated or in danger of being so in the near future? If by this we mean that population is outgrowing available space, we must consider another important factor: population density, or the number of people per square kilometre or per square mile. Viewed from this standpoint, it would be difficult to maintain that we are faced by global overpopulation now or in the foreseeable future.

As I have said, the number of people in the world today is 3,265 million. The land surface of the globe according to U.N. statistics is 135 million square kilometres. The population density —the average number of people per square kilometre—is therefore just over twenty-three. When this is adjusted to take into account Arctic wastes, mountains, forests, deserts and semi-arid land, the number of people per square kilometre of actually habitable, cultivable land is about 38 per square kilometre, or 88 per square mile. It is interesting to note that the population density of England and Wales, without making such an adjustment, is many times that amount at 309 per square kilometre or 792 per square mile. Recent figures for Holland give a population density of nearly 900 per square mile.[13]

There are in fact few areas that can be considered overpopulated. Africa as a whole has a population density of less than ten per square kilometre; Borneo and New Guinea, among the largest islands in the world, and most of Indonesia and Malaysia (except, of course, Java) are thinly populated. Indeed, Borneo is facing a crisis of depopulation and underpopulation. Australia, Canada and South America have very small populations. In fact, only one country of South America—Uruguay—has a population density of over 20 per square kilometre, and most are below ten. It must always be remembered that one of the elements of over-population is to be thickly populated.

On the other hand, there are population "blackspots" which,

[13] 356 per square kilometre.

due to the publicity they receive, are well known: India, with a rate of increase of 2.7% on a population of 460 million (i.e., 12.4 million per year), the West Indies, southern China, Java and parts of Central America. Of course it must be remembered that population density is a very rough yardstick unless, in very bad country, adjustments are made. Nevertheless, even in a mountainous country, such as Colombia, with an overall population density of 11 per square kilometre, the density adjusted to include good land alone is only 180, by no means excessive.

However, distribution of population must also be taken into account. In a relatively underpopulated country, there may still be areas of urban conurbations that are actually overpopulated; this is especially true of South American countries. For example, 10 million of Argentina's population of 21 million live in one or two big cities. This also applies to some parts of Africa, as well as to southern China and some others parts of the East and Far East.

1. *Examples of Some Low Population Densities*

	Population	Rate of Increase	Area in Sq. Km.	Density per Sq. Km.
AFRICA				
Cameroon	753,358	Not computed	475,442	11
Central African Republic	1,227,400	2.3	612,000	2
Congo (Brazzaville)	581,600	1.5	342,000	2
Kenya	8,636,263	3.5	322,463	11
Uganda	6,536,616	2.5	236,037	30
SOUTH AMERICA				
Bolivia	2,704,165	1.4	1,098,581	3
Chile	7,374,115	2.3	741,767	11
Colombia	11,548,172	2.2	1,138,338	13
Australia	10,508,186	2.1	7,695,094	1
New Zealand	2,414,984	2.2	268,676	9

2. Examples of Some High Population Densities

Japan	93,418,501	0.9	369,661	259
England	46,104,548	0.8	151,120	312
West Germany	53,977,418	1.3	247,973	224
Belgium	9,189,741	0.5	30,513	304
Netherlands	11,461,964	1.4	33,612	356
India	435,511,606	*2.3*[14]	3,046,232	151

It will be realized from what has been said that the population problem is much more complex than is sometimes indicated, even when we are considering only people and space as we have been doing so far. It really should be considered region by region, country by country, even district by district. The sweeping generalizations not uncommon in popular literature are deprecated by scientific population experts.

The situation becomes still more complex when the third essential element in assessing population problems is introduced, namely, food and economic resources, actual and potential, discovered and yet to be found, with relation to population density and rate of increase. This makes it almost impossible to give a clear-cut definition of overpopulation. *Present* regional overpopulation is relatively easy to recognize but not to define.

There are very large tracts of land even in the underdeveloped world which are seriously underpopulated and yet which have considerable habitable potential. West Africa, where I lived for a number of years, is a case in point. Taking former French West Africa, French Equatorial Africa and the Cameroons and Togoland, we get the following breakdown of land use:

Classification of Area	Number of Acres
Desert and Wasteland	500,000,000
Shifting Cultivation	175,000,000
Additional Land for Grazing	75,000,000
Not utilized at all	1,150,000,000
	1,900,000,000

[14] Italics indicate questionable reliability. I have given elsewhere in the article latest estimates for India, as this country has one of the most acute population problems.

However, in certain cases an average population density related to resources can give a false picture, especially in South America. For example, in Venezuela the population density and comparatively high average per capita income hide the real picture. The population increase of 2.7% is an average of a rate of about 1% for the prosperous classes and an extremely high 4% or 5% for the poor of Caracas, for example, who are almost completely unproductive, have little share in Venezuela's prosperity, and are "carried" by the comparatively small rich sector of the population.

Another reservation must also be made. Even in underpopulated countries a high rate of population increase—and anything over 1.5% must, in my opinion, be regarded as high in this context—does impose burdens which would be considerable even for developed countries. Where acute poverty exists, such high rates of increase can exert pressures on food supply and other economic resources that would be unbearable without considerable outside aid especially designed to take care of the problems resulting from rapid population expansion.

However, population pressures can also be viewed in a positive light: as an incentive to more rapid development, quicker social change and, in particular, the speeding up of the agricultural revolution which is absolutely necessary in most economically backward countries. However, we must beware of believing in the feasibility of "crash" agricultural programs undertaken without adequate knowledge and research. In areas of very rapid population growth combined with great poverty, and in cases of regional overpopulation such as the unhealthy urban conurbations of South America, for example, they cannot be expected to produce results unless population policies are worked out at the same time. Some form of limitation of births by acceptable means for the good of the community and for personal well-being is an urgent need. In one of the slums on the outskirts of Peru I saw a woman who had nine children, and she was not yet twenty-one years of age. She was living in a miserable shack without light or a water supply.

PEOPLE, SPACE AND FOOD

Bearing the above reservations in mind, it is well to realize, as I have indicated, that we are not faced with global overpopulation; in many cases we are faced with a serious population situation, but in many others there is underpopulation, and again in others the situation is serious only because of lack of agricultural and economic development. This helps to put into perspective views such as the following expressed by Fairfield Osborn in his introduction to *Our Crowded Planet*: "This book stems from the conviction that the inordinately rapid increase of populations in this world is the most essential problem which faces *everybody, everywhere.*"

To return to the relationship between people, space and food, it is often stressed that, although the population and food production levels in the world as a whole have been more or less in equilibrium over the last decade, in many poorer countries the race between population increase and food production is being lost. South America, with a population increase rate of 2.7%, has an agricultural productivity rate of only 1.6%, India shows similar figures.

First of all, it must be stated that there is no necessary connection between the two. The cause of the falling off of agricultural production is not population growth (except indirectly and only in some cases) but bad agriculture. In countries such as Pakistan, where priority has been given to investment in agriculture, and especially in training and education in improved agricultural techniques, the rate of increase in food production is 3.5%, while of population it is 2.7%. In Mexico, at one stage in its successful agricultural revolution in the last decade, food production was increasing at a rate of 7.2% per annum, while population increase was 2.7%. In fact, it could be said that where population increase is winning, it is *precisely because agricultural resources are not being developed.*

The agricultural surpluses of the developed countries, for technical and other reasons, do not provide complete solutions for lack of food in developing countries. They do, however, point to what can happen when technology is applied to farming methods. The importance of this is evident when it is realized that in large areas of the world the cause of lack of food, as well as a basic cause of poverty, is completely antiquated methods of subsistence farming attempting to feed rising populations.

This is obviously the view of Dr. Luis Bramao (head of the World Soil Office of the Land and Water Development Department of F.A.O.) who pointed out[15] that Holland with a high population density of 356 per square kilometre also has a high standard of living. In the United States in 1963, 75% more corn was produced on 27% fewer acres than twenty-five years previously. He added, giving point to his words: "There is only one inhabitant per square kilometre in Matto Grosso, Brazil's largest state, where the soil potential is tremendous. But who is going to cultivate it?"

Dr. Sen, Director General of F.A.O., in his report to the United Nations World Population Conference in Belgrade last year, said F.A.O.'s official position is that there is sufficient knowledge to bring about the increase needed in food production. To him, the problem lies primarily in social and institutional factors. These include: general neglect of farmers, lack of incentive, need for land reform, basic education and adequate credit and marketing facilities, massive investment in agriculture with much of it needing to come from foreign sources.

Dr. Sen warned that the situation would be critical for the coming two or three decades, adding, "We will either see the beginning of mankind as a whole taking responsibility for its destiny, or drift toward disaster. . . . Man, with his inexhaustible resources of intelligence and inventiveness, is capable of meeting the challenge."

What Dr. Sen says about food production applies to economic advance as a whole. However, population increase must be ac-

[15] To me in a conversation in Rome in November, 1965. He is engaged in the extremely valuable work of compiling a soil map of the world.

cepted as a very serious complication of the poverty existing in certain parts of the world. Since independence in 1947, India has increased its population by 100 million—a very considerable increase—and its rate of increase at 2.7% on a population of 460 million is over 12 million per year who are consuming non-producers. Nevertheless, the thesis remains true that the causes of poverty are much wider and that population increase cannot be used as a scapegoat for world poverty and lack of development. And if, by some miracle, tomorrow some absolutely effective, completely acceptable, cheap and readily applicable method of limiting population could immediately[16] be used to curtail births and population growth, the real causes of poverty would still remain to be tackled.

The conclusion is then that population pressures cause grave problems in some developing countries. The situation is not so grave as it has often been made out to be, but it is grave enough and it does very seriously complicate problems of development in some areas and therefore deserves urgent consideration.

The first effect of this consideration could well be expressed in the words of Paul Hoffman: "It will obviously take a long time for any serious impact to be made on the problem of excessively high rates of population increase. This makes all the more urgent the job of accelerating economic growth and social advancement in the underdeveloped world." [17] It is unlikely that any population measures will help in the crucial short term: hence the need for a much greater effort to increase food supplies and economic development of the poorer countries.[18]

The second effect should be increased research, undertaken in a scientific spirit, into the problems of demographic expansion, and action taken, where possible, to promote responsibility in

[16] Let us stress that so far such methods—useful in developing countries—do not seem in sight in spite of the latest devices.

[17] *World without Want* (London: Chatto & Windus), p. 666.

[18] India, e.g., allotted 64 million dollars to family planning in her first three plans. The population increase rate during that time rose from 1.3% per year or 5.1 million at the beginning (1951) to 2.7% in 1965.

parenthood by acceptable means which take into account the whole of family life and which do not depend simply on techniques.

In both these areas, the Church must employ competent experts in order to play her part,[19] a part based on thorough empirical knowledge enlightened and inspired by her sound moral doctrine, based on respect for life, for the dignity of the human person. In this field "a little knowledge is a dangerous thing". The section on population growth in the *Constitution on the Church in the Modern World* with its balanced approach and exhortation to further research is of great value for the Catholic demographer, and indeed for the whole science of demography.

Equally important are sections of Chapter 1 of Part II on marriage. The solution to the population explosion must come from a more responsible attitude to the sacred privilege of passing on new life. Even though methods of family planning still leave much to be desired from the point of view of acceptability, ease of use, safety, thorough clinical testing, cheapness and security, as much use as possible must be made of existing methods that are morally acceptable, and a crash program of research into new methods must be pursued with unremitting zeal. Obviously, the present rapid increase of population cannot be allowed to go on indefinitely, and it is completely naive in the new circumstances of lessened mortality rates to expect nature unaided to redress the balance.

[19] In my speech at the DO.C in Rome and in books and articles, I have developed at greater length what I think the role of the Church might be. See my books: *People, Space, Food* (London: Sheed & Ward, 1960); *The Population Explosion and World Hunger* (Burns & Oates, 1963) (American title: *World Poverty and the Christian*, New York); *Christian Responsibility and World Poverty* (Burns and Oates, 1963); see also SELIPO, the population secretariat of Louvain (Secrétariat pour liaison des études de la population), which was established in 1961 and has had yearly meetings and provides a coordinating service for Catholic demographers and other scientists throughout the world. Its role is to stimulate objective research into problems and their solution.

BIOGRAPHICAL NOTES

JOHN COURTNEY MURRAY, S.J.: Born September 12, 1905, in New York, he became a Jesuit and was ordained in 1933. He studied at Boston College, Woodstock College and the Gregorian University in Rome, earning his doctorate in theology in 1937. He was a lecturer in medieval philosophy at Yale University in 1951 and 1952, and is presently a lecturer in theology at Woodstock College. His published works include *We Hold These Truths* (1960) and *The Problem of God* (1964). He is editor of, as well as contributor to, *Theological Studies,* and co-editor of *American Ecclesiastical Review* and *America.* He has also written for the *Encyclopaedia Britannica.*

ROLAND BAINTON: Born March 30, 1894, in Ilkeston, Derbyshire, England, he was ordained in the Congregational Church. He studied at Yale University, earning his doctorate in theology in 1921. At one time he aided refugees, working under the auspices of the Society of Friends. At present he is a pastor in the United Church of Christ. Among his published works are *Here I Stand; A Life of Martin Luther* (1950), *Bernardino Ochimo* (1940), *David Joris—Anabaptist* and *Castellio concerning Heretics.* He is presently engaged on a study of the life of Erasmus.

C. JAIME SNOEK, C.SS.R.: Born December 25, 1920, in Mijdrecht, Holland, he became a Redemptorist and was ordained in 1947. He studied at the Pontifical Athenaeum Angelicum and earned his degree in theology in 1952. He occupies several posts at present. He is professor of moral and pastoral theology and professor of liturgy at the Redemptorist Seminary of Juiz de Fora, Brazil; he is also professor of moral sciences in the Faculty of Social Services, Juiz de Fora, and theological consultor for the Episcopal Conference and the Conference of Religious, Brazil. He is a regular contributor to many reviews, including *Revista Eclesiástica Brasileira.*

YVES CONGAR, O.P.: Born April 13, 1904, in Sedan, France, he became a Dominican and was ordained in 1930. He pursued his philosophical studies at the Institut Catholique in Paris and studied theology at Le Saulchoir in Etiolles, France. From 1931 to 1954 he was professor of fundamental theology and ecclesiology at Le Saulchoir. His published works are numerous and erudite. Among them are *Lay People in the Church* (1957), *After Nine Hundred Years* (1959), *Laity, Church and World* (1960), *The Mystery of the Church* (1960), *The Mystery of the Temple* (1962), and *The Meaning of Tradition* (1964).

ALOIS MÜLLER: Born September 20, 1924, in Basle, he was ordained in 1949. He studied theology and philosophy in Fribourg and in Rome, and earned his doctorate in theology in 1951. After several years in parish work, he taught religion for seven years in a Solothurn school. From 1959 to 1962 he took part, ultimately as director, in the pastoral study courses at the Solothurn seminary. After sabbatical leave for studies at Münster, Paris and Columbia University, New York, he became professor of pastoral theology at the University of Fribourg in 1964. His published works are in German, and an English translation of one of them, under the title of *Obedience in the Church,* will shortly be published by Newman Press of Westminster, Maryland. He contributes regularly to various reviews.

ALONZO-M. HAMELIN, O.F.M.: Born December 4, 1920, in S. Narcisse (diocese of Trois-Rivières), Canada, he became a Franciscan and was ordained in 1949. He studied at the Seminaire Saint Antoine in Trois Rivières, the Cléricat Théologique Franciscain in Montreal, and the Pontifical Athenaeum St. Antoine in Rome, earning his doctorate in theology. At one time professor of moral theology at the Cléricat Théologique Franciscain, he is at present lecturer at the University of Montreal. He has several published works in French to his credit, and is a regular contributor to various reviews. He is editor of *La vie des communautés religieuses.*

THEODORE L. WESTOW: Born June 17, 1908, in The Hague, he studied in Holland and at London University, becoming fluent in six languages. He has spent most of his life teaching, and at present is lecturer at the Salisbury and South Wilts College for Further Education. His extensive travels throughout Europe have included periods with the Protestant community of Taizé and with the priest-workers in Paris. In addition to writing and translating, he has broadcast for the B.B.C. on the part of the layman in the Church, and he is active in the United Nations Association and the Freedom from Hunger Campaign. His published works include *Who Is My Brother?, New Thinking on Sin, University of Mankind, Ecumenism,* and *The Variety of Catholic Attitudes* (New York: Herder and Herder, 1963). He is a regular contributor to *Life of the Spirit, Pax Romana Journal, The Layman,* and many other publications.

COENRAAD VAN OUWERKERK, C.SS.R.: Born July 15, 1923, in Hilversum, Holland, he became a Redemptorist and was ordained in 1948. He studied at the Angelicum, the Academia Alfonsiana in Rome, and the Catholic University of Nijmegen, Holland, earning his doctorate in theology in 1956. He is professor of moral theology and pastoral psychology at the Redemptorist House in Wittem, Holland, and is a member of the Pastoral Commission of the Katholieke Vereniging van Geestlijke Volksgezondheid. He contributes articles to a number of reviews and is the translator of the Dutch edition of Bernard Häring's *The Law of Christ* (Mercier Press).

FRANZ BÖCKLE: Born April 18, 1921, in Glarus, Switzerland, he was ordained in 1945 for the diocese of Coire. He studied at the Angelicum in Rome and at the University of Munich, earning his doctorate in theology in 1952. He has been a professor of moral theology in the seminary in Chur, Switzerland, and is at present professor at the University of Bonn, W. Germany. His published works deal with general ethical and moral problems (the ethics of the Evangelical Church, natural law and similar subjects).

ARTHUR MCCORMACK: Born August 16, 1911, in England, he joined the Mill Hill Fathers and was ordained in 1936. He studied at the University of Durham, earning his doctorate in history and economics. At one time Headmaster of St. John's College, West Cameroon, and professor at the African Training College, West Cameroon, he has been a lecturer in pastoral sociology at Mill Hill College since 1963. His many published works are concerned chiefly with the problems of population explosion, poverty and famine. They include *People, Space, Food* (1960), *Christian Responsibility and World Poverty* (1963), *World Poverty and the Christian* (1963), *Poverty and Population* (1964) and *Cardinal Vaughan* (1966).

International Publishers of CONCILIUM

ENGLISH EDITION
Paulist Press
Glen Rock, N. J., U.S.A.
Burns & Oates Ltd.
25 Ashley Place
London, S.W.1

GERMAN EDITION
Verlagsanstalt Benziger & Co., A.G.
Einsiedeln, Switzerland
Matthias Grunewald-Verlag
Mainz, W. Germany

DUTCH EDITION
Uitgeverij Paul Brand, N. V.
Hilversum, Netherlands

SPANISH EDITION
Ediciones Guadarrama
Madrid, Spain

FRENCH EDITION
Maison Mame
Tours/Paris, France

PORTUGUESE EDITION
Livraria Morais Editora, Ltda.
Lisbon, Portugal

ITALIAN EDITION
Editrice Queriniana
Brescia, Italy